SUPER
SCIENCE

SUPER SCIENCE

Steve Parker

Duncan Brewer

Miles
Kelly

First published in 2013 by Miles Kelly Publishing Ltd
Harding's Barn, Bardfield End Green, Thaxted, Essex, CM6 3PX, UK

2 4 6 8 10 9 7 5 3 1

Publishing Director Belinda Gallagher
Creative Director Jo Cowan
Editors Rosie McGuire, Sarah Parkin
Editorial Assistant Amy Johnson
Cover Designer Rob Hale
Designers Kayleigh Allen, Rob Hale
Production Manager Elizabeth Collins
Reprographics Stephan Davis, Jennifer Hunt, Lorraine King, Thom Allaway

ISBN 978-1-84810-907-0

Printed in China

British Library Cataloguing-in-Publication Data
A catalogue record for this book is available from the British Library

Made with paper from a sustainable forest

www.mileskelly.net   info@mileskelly.net

www.factsforprojects.com

CONTENTS

SCIENCE

INVENTIONS

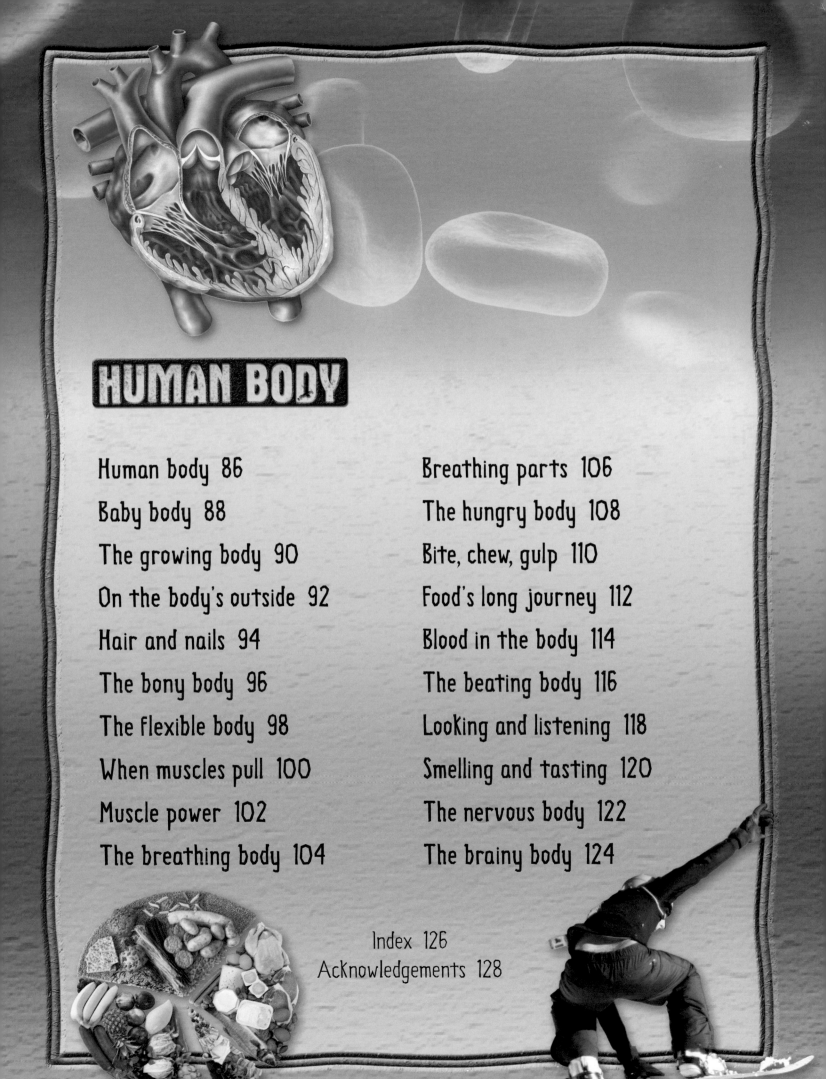

HUMAN BODY

Even one hundred books like this could not explain all the reasons why we need science. Toasters, bicycles, mobile phones, computers, cars, light bulbs – all the gadgets and machines we use every day are the results of scientific discoveries. Houses, skyscrapers, bridges and rockets are built using science. Our knowledge of medicines, nature, light and sound comes from science. Then there is the science of predicting the weather, investigating how stars shine, finding out why carrots are orange…

▼ In a big city, science is all around you — everything from sky-scraping buildings to speedy vehicles and useful gadgets is based on science and technology.

Machines big and small

Machines are everywhere! They help us do things, or make doing them easier. Every time you play on a see-saw, you are using a machine! A lever is a stiff bar that tilts at a point called the pivot or fulcrum. The pivot of the see-saw is in the middle. Using the see-saw as a lever, a small person can lift a big person by sitting further from the pivot.

▶ On a see-saw lever, the pivot is in the middle. Other levers have pivots at the end.

Thread

▶ Turning a screw moves it along with more force than the effort used to turn it.

The screw is another simple but useful scientific machine. It is a ridge, or thread, wrapped around a bar or pole. It changes a small turning motion into a powerful pulling or lifting movement. Wood screws hold together furniture or shelves. A car jack lets you lift up a whole car.

Where would you be without wheels? Not going very far. The wheel is a simple machine, a circular disc that turns around its centre on a bar called an axle. Wheels carry heavy weights easily. There are giant wheels on big trucks and trains and small wheels on rollerblades.

Axle

▼ Wheels reduce friction, allowing heavy loads to be carried more easily.

▼ Two pulleys together reduce the force needed to lift a heavy girder by one half.

▲ Bicycle gears mean you can pedal at the same speed, with the same force, when climbing up a hill or speeding down it.

Reversing gears

Sliding rack

Pinion gear

Bevel gears

Slow pinion gear

Screw-shaped worm gear

A pulley turns around, like a wheel. It has a groove around its edge for a cable or rope. Lots of pulleys allow us to lift very heavy weights easily. The pulleys on a tower crane can lift huge steel girders to the top of a skyscraper.

Pivot

Lever

▲ Gears change the turning direction of a force. They can slow it down or speed it up – and even convert it into a sliding force (rack and pinion).

I DON'T BELIEVE IT!

A ramp is a simple machine called an inclined plane. It is easier to walk up a ramp than to jump straight to the top.

Gears are like wheels, with pointed teeth around the edges. They change a fast, weak turning force into a slow, powerful one – or the other way around. On a bicycle, you can pedal up the steepest hill in bottom (lowest) gear, then speed down the other side in top (highest) gear.

When science is hot!

Fire! Flames! Burning! Heat! The science of heat is important in all kinds of ways. Not only do we cook with heat, but we also warm our homes and heat water. Burning happens in all kinds of engines in cars, trucks, planes and rockets. It is also used in factory processes, from making steel to shaping plastics.

▲ A firework burns suddenly as an explosive, producing heat, light and sound. The 'bang' is the sound made by the paper wrapper as it is blown apart.

Heat from the drink is conducted up the metal spoon

Heat can move by conduction. A hot object will pass on, or transfer, some of its heat to a cooler one. Dip a metal spoon in a hot drink and the spoon handle soon warms up. Heat is conducted from the drink, through the metal.

Heat moves by invisible 'heat rays'. This is called thermal radiation and the rays are infrared waves. Our planet is warmed by the Sun because heat from the Sun radiates through space as infrared waves.

TRUE OR FALSE?

1. Burning happens inside the engine of a plane.
2. A device for measuring temperature is called a calendar.
3. Heat rays are known as infrablue waves.

Answers:
1. True 2. False 3. False

◀ Metal is a good conductor of heat. Put a teaspoon in a hot drink and feel how quickly it heats up.

Burning, also called combustion, is a chemical process. Oxygen gas from the air joins to, or combines with, the substance being burned. The chemical change releases lots of heat, and usually light too. If this happens really fast, we call it an explosion.

▲ A burner flame makes glass so hot it becomes soft and bendy, so it can be stretched, shaped and even blown up like a balloon.

Temperature is a measure of how hot or cold something is. It is usually measured in degrees Celsius (°C) or Fahrenheit (°F). Water freezes at 0°C (32°F), and boils at 100°C (212°F). We use thermometers to take our temperatures. Your body temperature is about 37°C (98.6°F).

► This thermometer contains alcohol coloured by a red dye. As it warms, the alcohol expands (takes up more space). It moves up the thin tube, showing the temperature on the scale.

°C °F

Heat moves through liquids and gases by convection. Some of the liquid or gas takes in heat, gets lighter, and rises into cooler areas. Then other cooler liquid or gas moves in to do the same and the process repeats. You can see this as 'wavy' hot air rising from a flame.

► Hot air shimmering over a candle is a visible sign of the heat being convected away.

13

Engine power

Imagine having to walk or run everywhere, instead of riding in a car. Engines are machines that use fuel to do work for us and make life easier. Fuel is a substance that has chemical energy stored inside it. The energy is released as heat by burning or exploding the fuel in the engine.

Turbines squash incoming air

▼ A jet engine has sets of angled blades, called turbines, that spin on shafts.

Jet fuel is sprayed into the air inside the chamber, creating a small explosion

Burning gases spin exhaust turbines

Most cars have petrol engines. An air and petrol mixture is pushed into a hollow chamber called a cylinder. A spark from a spark plug makes it explode, which pushes a piston down inside the cylinder. This movement is used by gears to turn the wheels. Most cars have four or six cylinders.

A diesel engine doesn't use sparks. The mixture of air and diesel is squashed in the cylinder, becoming so hot it explodes. Diesel engines are used in machines such as tractors that need lots of power.

▼ This shows the four-stroke cycle of a petrol engine.

① Air and petrol mixture is sucked into the cylinder

② The piston moves up and squeezes the mixture

③ A spark from the plug makes the mixture explode

④ The piston rises to push waste gases out of the cylinder

Air and petrol

Inlet valve open

Rotating shaft

Piston moves down

Air and petrol are squeezed

Piston moves up

Exhaust valve open

Spark plug fires

Piston pushed down

▲ On a fast jet plane at full power, the exhaust gases from the engines glow almost white-hot.

A jet engine mixes air and kerosene and sets fire to it in one long, continuous, roaring explosion. Incredibly hot gases blast out of the back of the engine. These push the engine forward – along with the plane.

An electric motor passes electricity through coils of wire. This makes the coils magnetic, and they push or pull against magnets around them. The push-pull makes the coils spin on their shaft (axle).

Engines that burn fuel give out gases and particles through their exhausts. Some of these gases are harmful to the environment. The less we use engines, the better. Electric motors are quiet, efficient and reliable, but they still need fuel – to make the electricity at the power station.

▲ Electric cars have sets of batteries to turn the motor. The batteries are 'filled' with electrical energy by plugging into a recharging point.

▼ Using magnetic forces, an electric motor turns electrical energy into moving or kinetic energy.

Battery

Spinning contact (commutator)

Current flows along wire

Magnet

QUIZ

1. Are exhaust gases good for the environment?

2. Does a diesel engine use sparks?

3. How many cylinders do most cars have?

4. Do electric cars have batteries?

Answers:
1. No, some of them are harmful
2. No 3. Four or six 4. Yes

Science on the move

Without science, you would have to walk everywhere, or ride a horse. Luckily, scientists and engineers have developed many methods of transport, most importantly, the car. Lots of people can travel together in a bus, train, plane or ship. These use less energy and resources, and make less pollution than cars.

▼ Modern airports are enormous. They can stretch for several miles, and they have a constant flow of planes taking off and landing. Hundreds of people are needed to make sure that everything runs smoothly and on time.

Passenger terminal

Jetway

Science is used to stop criminals. Science-based security measures include a 'door frame' that detects metal objects like guns and a scanner that sees inside bags. A sniffer-machine can detect the smell of explosives or illegal drugs.

QUIZ
1. How do air traffic controllers talk to pilots?
2. What does a red train signal mean?
3. What powers the supports that move jetways?

Answers:
1. By radio 2. Stop 3. Electric motors

16

Every method of transport needs to be safe and on time. In the airport control tower, air traffic controllers track planes on radar screens. They talk to pilots by radio. Beacons send out radio signals, giving the direction and distance to the airport.

Jetways are extending walkways that stretch out from the passenger terminal right to the planes' doors. Their supports move along on wheeled trolleys driven by electric motors.

▶ The radar screen shows each aircraft as a blip, with its flight number or identity code.

On the road, drivers obey traffic lights. On a railway network, train drivers obey similar signal lights of different colours, such as red for stop. Sensors by the track record each train passing and send the information by wires or radio to the control room. Each train's position is shown as a flashing light on a wall map.

▼ Train signals show just two colours – red for stop and green for go.

D-27

▶ Trackside switches and detectors react to a train going past and automatically change the signals, so that a following train does not get too close.

Noisy science

Listening to the radio or television, playing music, shouting at each other – they all depend on the science of sound – acoustics. Sounds are carried by invisible waves in the air. The waves are areas of low pressure, where air particles are stretched farther apart, alternating with areas of high pressure, where they are squashed closer together.

5. Ship's computer displays information

1. Ship emits sound waves or tows sonar probe

2. Probe emits sound waves

3. Sound waves bounce off surfaces such as seabed

4. Echoes (reflected waves) detected by probe

Scientists measure the loudness or intensity of sound in decibels, dB. A very quiet sound like a ticking watch is 10 dB. Ordinary speech is 50–60 dB. Loud music is 90 dB. A jet plane taking off is 120 dB. Too much noise damages the ears.

◀ In sonar (echo–sounding), sound waves in the water bounce or reflect off objects, and are detected.

Atomic explosion

Whether a sound is high or low is called its pitch, or frequency. It is measured in Hertz, Hz. A singing bird or whining motorcycle has a high pitch. A rumble of thunder or a massive truck has a low pitch. People can hear frequencies from 25 to 20,000 Hz.

Jet plane

Express train

Whisper

▶ The decibel scale measures the intensity, or energy, in sound.

0 dB   40 dB   80 dB   120 dB   180 dB

Sound waves spread out from a vibrating object that is moving rapidly to and fro. Stretch an elastic band between your fingers and twang it. As it vibrates, it makes a sound. When you speak, vocal cords in your neck vibrate. You can feel them through your skin.

Sound waves travel about 330 metres every second. This is fast, but it is one million times slower than light waves. Sound waves also bounce off hard, flat surfaces. This is called reflection. The returning waves are heard as an echo.

Loudspeakers change electrical signals into sounds. The signals in the wire pass through a wire coil inside the speaker. This turns the coil into a magnet, which pushes and pulls against another magnet. The pushing and pulling make the cone vibrate, which sends sound waves into the air.

◄ The word 'sonic' means making sounds, and the high-pitched noises of bats can be described as 'ultrasonic' – too high for us to hear.

Echoes bouncing back off the moth

Sound waves from the bat

▲ Bats make high-pitched sounds. If the sounds hit an insect they bounce back to the bat's ears. The reflected sound (echo) gives the bat information about the size and location of the insect.

BOX GUITAR

You will need:

shoebox   elastic band
split pins   card

Cut a hole about 10 centimetres across on one side of an empty shoebox. Push split pins through either side of the hole, and stretch an elastic band between them. Pluck the band. Hear how the air and box vibrate. Cover the hole with card. Is the 'guitar' as loud?

Look out – light's out!

Almost everything you do depends on light and the science of light, which is called optics. Light is a form of energy that you can see. Light waves are made of electricity and magnetism – and they are tiny. About 2000 of them laid end to end would stretch across this full stop.

Light is directed back, giving a back-to-front reflection

Light waves hit mirror

▲ Light waves hit a mirror and are directed back, giving a back-to-front reflected view of the object.

▲ A prism of clear glass or clear plastic separates the colours in white light.

Like sound, light bounces off surfaces that are very smooth. This is called reflection. A mirror is smooth, hard and flat. When you look at it, you see your reflection.

Ordinary light from the Sun or from a light bulb is called white light. But when white light passes through a prism, a triangular block of clear glass, it splits into many colours. These colours are known as the spectrum. Each colour has a different length of wave. A rainbow is made by raindrops, which work like millions of tiny prisms to split up sunlight.

Light passes through certain materials, like clear glass and plastic. Materials that let light pass through, to give a clear view, are transparent. Those that do not allow light through, like wood and metal, are opaque.

Mirrors and lenses are important parts of many optical (light-using) gadgets. They are found in cameras, binoculars, microscopes, telescopes and lasers. Without them, we would have no close-up photographs of tiny microchips or insects or giant planets – in fact, no photos at all.

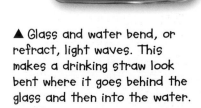

I DON'T BELIEVE IT!

Light is the fastest thing in the Universe – it travels through space at 300,000 kilometres per second. That's seven times around the world in less than one second!

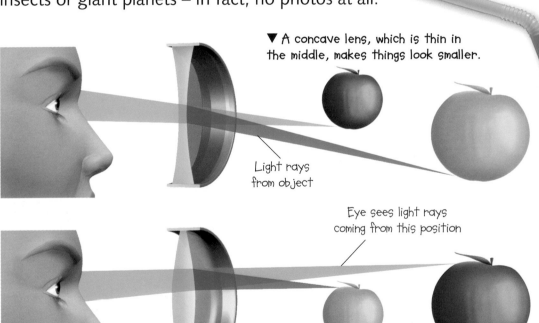

▼ A concave lens, which is thin in the middle, makes things look smaller.

Light rays from object

Eye sees light rays coming from this position

▲ A convex lens, which bulges in the middle, makes things look larger.

Light does not usually go straight through glass. It bends slightly where it goes into the glass, then bends back as it comes out. This is called refraction. A lens is a curved piece of glass or plastic that bends light to make things look bigger, smaller or clearer. Spectacle and contact lenses bend light to help people see more clearly.

▲ Glass and water bend, or refract, light waves. This makes a drinking straw look bent where it goes behind the glass and then into the water.

The power of lasers

Laser light is a special kind of light. Like ordinary light, it is made of waves, but it has three main differences. Ordinary white light is a mixture of colours, while laser light is one pure colour. Ordinary light waves have peaks (highs) and troughs (lows), which do not line up – laser light waves line up perfectly. Lastly, ordinary light spreads and fades. A laser beam can travel for thousands of kilometres as a strong, straight beam.

◀ The narrow horizontal beam from a laser spirit level can shine all the way across a building site.

▼ Waves of light build up and bounce to and fro inside a laser, then emerge at one end.

Silver mirror

Part-silver mirror

Particles in ruby crystal

Laser beam emerges

To make a laser beam, energy is fed in short bursts into a substance called the active medium. The energy might be electricity, heat or ordinary light. In a red ruby laser, the active medium is a rod of ruby crystal. A strong lamp makes the particles in the crystal vibrate. The energy they give off bounces to and fro inside the crystal. Eventually, the rays vibrate with each other and they are all the same length. The energy becomes so strong that it bursts through a mirror at one end of the crystal.

Beam bounces off CD

Laser

Spinning CD

Laser beam bent by prism

Reflected beam passes through prism

Reflected beam detected by sensor

▲ A CD laser detects tiny pits in the disc's underside.

▲ In a spectacular outdoor light show, different coloured laser beams sweep to and fro as they pierce the darkness, seemingly all the way into space.

Lasers were invented in 1960. They are used to play CDs and DVDs for music and movies, and in computers. They cut through thick metal in factories, and carry out delicate eye operations. They carry phone calls and television programmes along cables. They even measure movements of the Earth to warn of volcanoes or earthquakes.

QUIZ

1. How far can laser beams travel?

2. When were lasers invented?

3. Which everyday machines use lasers?

Answers:
1. Thousands of kilometres
2. 1960 3. DVD players, CD players, computers

◀ An industrial laser has the power to melt metal into gas and cut a neat line.

Mysterious magnets

Without magnets there would be no electric motors, computers or loudspeakers. Magnetism is an invisible force to do with atoms – tiny particles that make up everything. Atoms are made of even smaller particles, including electrons. Magnetism is linked to the way that these line up and move. Most magnetic substances contain iron. As iron makes up a big part of the metallic substance steel, steel is also magnetic.

▶ For metal recycling, an electromagnet lifts out only iron-containing or ferrous metals, such as steel.

A magnet is a lump of iron or steel that has all its electrons and atoms lined up. This means that their magnetic forces all add up. The force surrounds the magnet, in a region called the magnetic field. This is strongest at the two parts of the magnet called the poles.

▲ Maglev (magnetic levitation) trains use pushing or repelling magnetic forces to 'float' above their track.

A magnet has two different poles – north and south. A north pole repels (pushes away) the north pole of another magnet. Two south poles also repel each other. But a north pole and a south pole attract (pull together). Both magnetic poles attract any substance containing iron, like a nail or a screw.

When electricity flows through a wire, it makes a weak magnetic field around it. If the wire is wrapped into a coil, the magnetism becomes stronger. This is called an electromagnet. Its magnetic force is the same as an ordinary magnet, but when the electricity goes off, the magnetism does too. Some electromagnets are so strong, they can lift whole cars.

▼ The field around a magnet affects objects that contain iron.

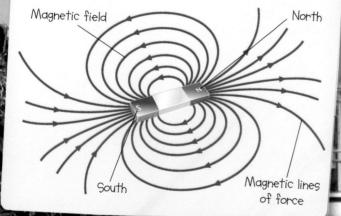

Magnetic field

North

South

Magnetic lines of force

QUIZ

Which of these substances or objects is magnetic?

1. Steel spoon 2. Plastic spoon
3. Pencil 4. Drinks can
5. Food can 6. Screwdriver
7. Cooking foil

Answers:
1. Yes 2. No 3. No 4. No 5. Yes 6. Yes 7. No

Electric sparks!

Flick a switch and things happen. The television goes off, the computer comes on, lights shine and music plays. Electricity is our favourite form of energy. We send it along wires and plug hundreds of machines into it.

▼ When an electric current flows, the electrons (small blue balls) all move the same way, jumping from one atom to the next. (The red balls are the centres or nuclei of the atoms.)

Electricity depends on electrons. In certain substances, when electrons are 'pushed', they hop from one atom to the next. When billions do this every second, electricity flows. The 'push' is from a battery or a generator. Electricity only flows in a complete loop or circuit. Break the circuit and the flow stops.

Atom

Electron

▼ Solar panels contain many hundreds of fingernail-sized PV (photovoltaic) cells. These convert light energy ('photo') to electrical energy ('voltaic').

▼ A battery has a chemical paste inside its metal casing.

Positive contact

Negative contact on base

A battery makes electricity from chemicals. Two different chemicals next to each other, such as an acid and a metal, swap electrons and get the flow going. Electricity's pushing strength is measured in volts. Most batteries are about 1.5, 3, 6 or 9 volts, with 12 volts in cars.

Electricity flows easily through some substances, including water and metals. These are electrical conductors. Other substances do not allow electricity to flow. They are insulators. Insulators include wood, plastic, glass, card and ceramics. Metal wires and cables have coverings of plastic, to stop the electricity leaking away.

Electricity from power stations is carried along cables on high pylons, or buried underground. This is known as the distribution grid. At thousands of volts, this electricity is extremely dangerous. For use in the home, it is changed to 220 volts (in the UK).

▼ Electricity generators are housed in huge casings, some bigger than trucks.

Pylon holds cables off the ground

◄ To check and repair high-voltage cables, the electricity must be turned off well in advance.

Mains electricity is made at a power station. A fuel such as coal or oil is burned to heat water into high-pressure steam. The steam pushes past the blades of a turbine and makes them spin. The turbines turn generators, which have wire coils near powerful magnets, and the spinning motion makes electricity flow in the coils.

MAKE A CIRCUIT

You will need:
lightbulb   battery   wire
plastic ruler   metal spoon   dry card

Join a bulb to a battery with pieces of wire, as shown. Electricity flows round the circuit and lights the bulb. Make a gap in the circuit and put various objects into it, to see if they allow electricity to flow again. Try a plastic ruler, a metal spoon and some dry card.

Making sounds and pictures

The air is full of waves we cannot see or hear, unless we have the right machine. Radio waves are a form of electrical and magnetic energy, just like heat and light waves, microwaves and X-rays. All of these are called electromagnetic waves and they travel at an equal speed – the speed of light.

Satellite

Radio waves

Radio waves carry their information by being altered, or modulated, in a certain pattern. The height of a wave is called its amplitude. If this is altered, it is known as AM (amplitude modulation). Look for AM on the radio display.

Radio waves are used for both radio and television. They travel vast distances. Long waves curve around the Earth's surface. Short waves bounce between the Earth and the sky.

Aerial

The number of waves per second is called the frequency. If this is altered, it is known as FM (frequency modulation). FM radio is clearer than AM, and less affected by weather and thunderstorms.

▼ This range of waves, with different wavelengths, are electrical and magnetic energy. They are called the electromagnetic spectrum.

▲ A radio set picks up radio waves using its aerial or antenna.

| Long radio waves | Shorter radio waves (TV) | Microwaves | Infrared waves | Light waves (visible light) | Ultraviolet rays | X-rays | Short X-rays | Gamma rays |

Radio waves are sent out, or transmitted, from antennae on tall masts or on satellites, to reach a very wide area. A radio receiver converts the pattern of waves to sounds. A television receiver or TV set changes them to pictures and sounds.

▼ A dish-shaped receiver picks up radio waves for TV channels.

I DON'T BELIEVE IT!

You could send and receive radio signals on the Moon, but not in the sea. Radio waves travel easily through space, but only a few metres in water.

Digital radio uses incredibly short bursts of radio waves with gaps between them — many thousands each second. Each burst represents the digit (number) 1, and a gap is 0. The order of the 1s and 0s carries information in the form of binary code, as in a computer.

▶ A plasma screen has thousands of tiny boxes, or cells, of three colours — red, green and blue. Electric pulses heat the gas inside for a split second into plasma, which gives out a burst of light. Combinations of these colours gives all the other colours.

▼ Flat-screen TVs can be LCD or plasma. They use less electricity than cathode-ray TVs and produce a better picture.

KEY
① Glowing 'on' cell
② Dark 'off' cell
③ Rear grid of electrical contacts
④ – ⑥ Coloured phosphors inside cells
⑦ Backing plate
⑧ Front grid of electrical contacts
⑨ Transparent front cover

Compy-science

Computers are amazing machines, but they have to be told exactly what to do. So we put in instructions and information, by various means. These include typing on a keyboard, inserting a disc or memory stick, downloading from the Internet, using a joystick or games controller, or linking up a camera, scanner or another computer.

Most computers are controlled by instructions from a keyboard and a mouse. The mouse moves a pointer around on the screen and its click buttons select choices from lists called menus.

Flat screen monitor

USB (Universal Serial Bus) sockets

External monitor (screen) socket

Headphone socket

Silicon 'wafer'

Plastic casing

◄ This close up of a slice of silicon 'wafer' shows the tiny parts that receive and send information in a computer.

Wire 'feet' link to other part in the computer

Some computers are controlled by talking to them! They pick up the sounds using a microphone. This is speech recognition technology.

The 'main brain' of a computer is its Central Processing Unit. It is usually a microchip – millions of electronic parts on a chip of silicon, hardly larger than a fingernail. It receives information and instructions from other microchips, carries out the work, and sends back the results.

▲ Launched in 2010, the Apple iPad began a new trend in computerized devices called 'tablets'.

QUIZ

You may have heard of these sets of letters. Do you know what they mean? Their full written-out versions are all here on these two pages.

1. RAM 2. ROM
3. CPU

Answers:
1. Random Access Memory
2. Read Only Memory
3. Central Processing Unit

CD or DVD drive reader

Mouse pad

Keyboard

▼ The keys on a keyboard have bendy metal contacts that come together when pressed, allowing electricity to flow.

Top flexible layer

Finger presses down on keypad

Conductive strips (red) not touching – circuit is open (incomplete)

Conductive strips make contact and complete circuit

◀ As well as desktop computers, there are also laptops with a fold-up LCD (liquid crystal display) screen. Touching the mouse pad with a finger controls the cursor or insert point on the screen.

Information and instructions are contained in the computer in memory microchips. There are two kinds. Random Access Memory is like a jotting pad. It keeps changing as the computer carries out its tasks. Read Only Memory is like an instruction book. It usually contains the instructions for how the computer starts up and how all the microchips work together.

A computer usually displays its progress on a monitor screen. It feeds information to output devices such as printers, loudspeakers and robot arms. Information can be stored on CDs, DVDs, memory sticks (chips), external HDs (hard drive discs), or uploaded to the Internet.

Web around the world

The world is at your fingertips – if you are on the Internet. The Internet is one of the most amazing results of science. It is a worldwide network of computers, linked like one huge electrical spider's web.

Signals travel between computers in many ways. These include electricity along telephone wires, flashes of laser light along fibre-optic cables or radio waves between tall towers. Information is changed from one form to another in a split second. It can also travel between computers on different sides of the world in less than a second using satellite links.

First 'private' Internet, ARPANET, for the US military

Joint Academic Network (JANET) connects UK universities via their own Internet

Yahoo! Launches as a 'Guide to the World Wide Web' – what we now call a browser or search engine

Animation starts to become common on websites

1969   **1984**   **1994**   **1996**

1961   **1972**   **1989**   **1995**

First ideas for 'packet switching', the basic way the Internet parcels up and sends information in small blocks or packets

First emails, mostly on ARPANET

The birth of the Internet as we know it today, when Tim Berners-Lee and the team at CERN invent the World Wide Web to make information easier to publish and access

eBay and Amazon booksellers begin, and online trade starts to rise

The World Wide Web is public information that anyone can find on the Internet, available for everyone to see. However, sometimes you have to pay or join a club to get to certain parts of it. A website is a collection of related information, usually made up of text, videos and pictures. There might be hundreds of web pages within each website. Email is the system for sending private messages from one person to another.

I DON'T BELIEVE IT!

The World Wide Web is the best known and most widely used part of the Internet system. It has billions of pages of information.

▼ Many mobile phones can be used to access the Internet, allowing users to browse web pages, send emails and watch videos.

Facebook has fewer new users signing up — is the slower growth temporary, or the beginning of the end for online social networking?

Half of households in the UK have Internet connections

YouTube is launched, allowing video sharing

The first iPhones bring mobile Internet use for almost anyone

2003   **2005**   **2007**   **2011**

1998   **2004**   **2006**   **2010**

Google is launched as a rival to Yahoo!

Facebook is launched, starting the trend for social networking over the Internet

Twitter is launched for posting and sharing text messages, but has a slow start

HD (High Definition) Internet video links become more practical

▲ The Web and the Internet interact with other technologies. Twitter is an online public version of text-only messages called 'tweets' developed from mobile phone 'texting' (SMS, Short Message Service).

What's it made of?

You wouldn't make a bridge out of straw, or a cup out of bubblewrap! Choosing the right substance for the job is important. All the substances in the world can be divided into several groups. For example, metals such as iron, silver and gold are strong, hard and shiny, and conduct heat and electricity well. They are used to make things that have to be strong and long-lasting.

Plastics are made mainly from the substances in petroleum (crude oil). There are so many kinds – some are hard and brittle while others are soft and bendy. They are usually long-lasting, not affected by weather or damp, and they resist heat and electricity.

KEY

1. The front wing is a special shape – this produces a force that presses the car down onto the track

2. The main body of the car is made from carbon fibre, a light but very strong material

3. The car's axles are made from titanium – a very strong, light metal

4. The engine is made from various alloys, or mixtures of metals, based on aluminium. It produces up to ten times the power of a family car engine

5. Each tyre is made of thick, tough rubber to withstand high speeds

6. The rear wing is also carbon fibre composite

▼ A racing car has thousands of parts made from hundreds of materials. Each is suited to certain conditions such as stress, temperature and vibrations.

Ceramics are materials based on clay or other substances dug from the Earth. They can be shaped and dried, like a clay bowl. Or they can be fired – baked in a hot oven called a kiln. This makes them hard and long-lasting, but brittle and prone to cracks. Ceramics resist heat and electricity very well.

Metal

Fibre

Ceramic

▲ Metal, fibre and ceramic can combine to make a composite material. The way all of these ingredients are arranged can affect the composite's strength.

◄ In 2007, the Interstate 35W bridge collapsed in Minneapolis, USA, killing 13 people. It was due to cracking of small steel connecting plates that were too thin for the weight.

Glass is produced from the raw substances limestone and sand. When heated at a high temperature, these substances become a clear, gooey liquid, which sets hard as it cools. Its great advantage is that you can see through it.

Composites are mixtures or combinations of different materials. For example, glass strands are coated with plastic to make GRP – glass-reinforced plastic. This composite has the advantages of both materials.

MAKE YOUR OWN COMPOSITE

You will need:
flour   newspaper strips
water   balloon   pin

You can make a composite called pâpier maché from flour, newspaper and water. Tear newspaper into strips. Mix flour and water into a paste. Dip each strip in the paste and place it around a blown-up balloon. Cover the balloon and allow it to dry. Pop the balloon with a pin, and the composite should stay in shape.

World of chemicals

The world is made of chemical substances. Some are completely pure. Others are mixtures of substances – such as petroleum (crude oil). Petroleum provides us with thousands of different chemicals and materials, such as plastics, paints, soaps and fuels. It is one of the most useful, and valuable, substances in the world.

The fumes cool as they rise up the tower, causing them to condense

Fuel gases for burning

Petrol and vehicle fuels

Kerosene and medium fuels (jet fuel)

Heavy oils for lubrication

Waxes, tars, bitumens, asphalts

Furnace

▼ The biggest offshore oil platforms are more than 150 metres tall above the ocean surface. They drill boreholes into the seabed and pump up the crude oil, or petroleum.

Crude oil is super-heated and some parts turn into fumes

▲ The huge tower (fractionating column) of an oil refinery may be 100 metres high.

In an oil refinery, crude oil is heated in a huge tower. Some of its different substances turn into fumes and rise up the tower. The fumes condense (turn back into liquids) at different heights inside, due to the different temperatures at each level. Thick, gooey tars, asphalts and bitumens – used to make road surfaces – remain at the bottom.

One group of chemicals is called acids. They vary in strength from very weak citric acid, which gives the sharp taste to fruits such as lemons, to extremely strong and dangerous sulphuric acid in a car battery. Powerful acids burn and corrode, or eat away, substances. Some even corrode glass or steel.

Another group of chemicals is bases. They vary in strength from weak alkaloids, which give the bitter taste to coffee beans, to strong and dangerous bases in drain cleaners and industrial polishes. Bases feel soapy or slimy and, like acids, they can burn or corrode.

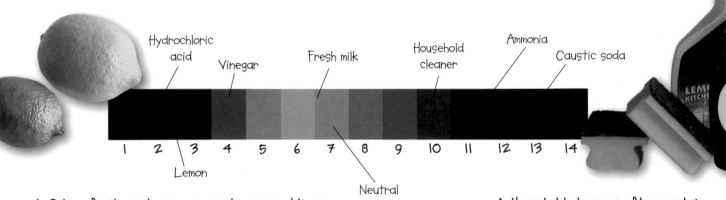

Hydrochloric acid | Vinegar | Fresh milk | Household cleaner | Ammonia | Caustic soda

1 2 3 4 5 6 7 8 9 10 11 12 13 14

Lemon

Neutral

▲ Citrus fruits such as oranges, lemons and limes have a tart taste because they contain a mild acid, called citric acid. It has a pH of 3.

▲ Household cleaners often contain alkalis to help them break down grease and fat. Some cleaners have a pH of 10.

Acidic substance

Neutral substance

Alkaline substance

▶ Indicator paper changes colour when it touches different substances. Acids turn it red, alkalis make it bluish–purple. The deeper the colour, the stronger the acid or base.

FROTHY FUN

You will need:
vinegar   washing soda

Create a chemical reaction by adding a few drops of vinegar to a spoonful of washing soda in a saucer. The vinegar is an acid, the soda is a base. The two react by frothing and giving off bubbles of carbon dioxide gas. What is left is a salt (but not to be eaten).

Acids and bases are 'opposite' types of chemicals. When they meet, they undergo changes called a chemical reaction. The result is usually a third type of chemical, called a salt. The common salt we use for cooking is one example. Its chemical name is sodium chloride.

Pure science

The world seems to be made of millions of different substances — such as soil, wood, concrete, plastics and air. These are combinations of simpler substances. If you could take them apart, you would see that they are made of pure substances called elements.

1	2	3	4	5	6	7	8	9	10	11	12
1 H Hydrogen											
3 Li Lithium	4 Be Beryllium										
11 Na Sodium	12 Mg Magnesium										
19 K Potassium	20 Ca Calcium	21 Sc Scandium	22 Ti Titanium	23 V Vanadium	24 Cr Chromium	25 Mn Manganese	26 Fe Iron	27 Co Colbalt	28 Ni Nickel	29 Cu Copper	30 Zn Zinc
37 Rb Rubidium	38 Sr Strontium	39 Y Yttrium	40 Zr Zirconium	41 Nb Niobium	42 Mo Molybdenum	43 Tc Technetium	44 Ru Ruthenium	45 Rh Rhodium	46 Pd Palladium	47 Ag Silver	48 Cd Cadmium
55 Cs Caesium	56 Ba Barium	Elements 57–71	72 Hf Hafnium	73 Ta Tantalum	74 W Tungsten	75 Re Rhenium	76 Os Osmium	77 Ir Iridium	78 Pt Platinum	79 Au Gold	80 Hg Mercury
87 Fr Francium	88 Ra Radium	Elements 89–103	104 Rf Rutherfordium	105 Db Dubnium	106 Sg Seaborgium	107 Bh Bohrium	108 HS Hassium	109 Mt Meitnerium	110 Ds Darmstadtium	111 Rg Roentgenium	112 Cn Copernicum

Atomic number → 20 Ca Calcium ← Chemical symbol / Name

57 La Lanthanum	58 Ce Cerium	59 Pr Praseodymium	60 Nd Neodymium	61 Pm Promethium	62 Sm Samarium	63 Eu Europium	64 Gd Gadolinium	65 Tb Terbium
89 Ac Actinium	90 Th Thorium	91 Pa Protactinium	92 U Uranium	93 Np Neptunium	94 Pu Plutonium	95 Am Americium	96 Cm Curium	97 Bk Berkelium

▶ Stars are made mainly of burning hydrogen, which is why they are so hot and bright.

▲ The Periodic Table is a chart of all the elements. In each row the atoms get heavier from left to right. Each column (up–down) contains elements with similar chemical features. Every element has a chemical symbol, name, and atomic number, which is the number of particles called protons in its central part, or nucleus.

Hydrogen is the simplest element and it is the first in the Periodic Table. This means it has the smallest atoms. It is a very light gas, which floats upwards in air. Hydrogen was used to fill giant airships. But there was a problem — hydrogen catches fire easily and explodes.

About 90 elements are found naturally on and in the Earth. In an element, all of its particles, called atoms, are exactly the same as each other. Just as important, they are all different from the atoms of any other element.

Element types

■ Alkali metals	■ Halogens
□ Alkaline metals	■ Inert gases
■ Transition metals	■ Lanthanides
■ Other metals	■ Actinides
■ Other non-metals	■ Trans-actinides

Note: Elements 113–118 are synthetic elements that have only been created briefly, so their properties cannot be known for certain.

				18	
					2 He Helium

13	14	15	16	17	
5 B Boron	6 C Carbon	7 N Nitrogen	8 O Oxygen	9 F Fluorine	10 Ne Neon
13 Al Aluminium	14 Si Silicon	15 P Phosphorus	16 S Sulphur	17 Cl Chlorine	18 Ar Argon
31 Ga Gallium	32 Ge Germanium	33 As Arsenic	34 Se Selenium	35 Br Bromine	36 Kr Krypton
49 In Indium	50 Sn Tin	51 Sb Antimony	52 Te Tellurium	53 I Iodine	54 Xe Xenon
81 Ti Thallium	82 Pb Lead	83 Bi Bismuth	84 Po Polonium	85 At Astatine	86 Rn Radon
113 Uut Ununtrium	114 Uuq Ununquadum	115 Uup Ununpentium	116 Uuh Ununhexium	117 Uus Ununsectium	118 Uuo Ununoctium

66 Dy Dysprosium	67 Ho Holmium	68 Er Erbium	69 As Arsenic	70 Yb Ytterbium	71 Lu Lutetium
98 Cf Californium	99 Es Einsteinium	100 Fm Fermium	101 Md Mendelevium	102 No Nobelium	103 Lr Lawrencium

QUIZ

1. How many elements are found naturally on Earth?
2. Which lightweight metal is very useful?
3. Which element makes up stars?
4. What do diamonds and coal have in common?

Answers:
1. About 90 2. Aluminium 3. Hydrogen 4. They are both made of pure carbon

Uranium is a heavy and dangerous element. It gives off harmful rays and tiny particles. This process is called radioactivity and it can cause sickness, burns and diseases such as cancer. Radioactivity is a form of energy and, under careful control, radioactive elements are used as fuel in nuclear power stations.

▶ Aluminium is a strong but light metal that is ideal for forming the body of vehicles such as planes.

Carbon is a very important element in living things — including our own bodies. It joins easily with atoms of other elements to make large groups of atoms called molecules. When it is pure, carbon can be two different forms. These are soft, powdery soot, and hard, glittering diamond. The form depends on how the carbon atoms join to each other.

Aluminium is an element that is a metal, and it is one of the most useful in modern life. It is light and strong, it does not rust, and it is resistant to corrosion. Saucepans, drinks cans, cooking foil and jet planes are made mainly of aluminium.

Bond (link)   Atom

◀ Diamond is a form of the element carbon where the atoms are linked, or bonded, in a very strong box-like pattern.

Small science

Many pages in this book mention atoms. They are the smallest bits of a substance. They are so tiny, even a billion atoms would be too small to see. But scientists have carried out experiments to find out what's inside an atom. The answer is – even smaller bits. These are sub-atomic particles, and there are three main kinds.

At the centre of each atom is a blob called the nucleus. It contains two kinds of sub-atomic particles. These are protons and neutrons. Protons are positive, or plus. The neutron is neither positive nor negative. Around the centre of each atom are sub–atomic particles called electrons. They whizz round the nucleus. In the same way that a proton in the nucleus is positive or plus, an electron is negative or minus. The number of protons and electrons is usually the same.

I DON'T BELIEVE IT!

One hundred years ago, people thought the electrons were spread out in an atom, like the raisins in a raisin pudding.

Atoms of the various elements have different numbers of protons and neutrons. An atom of hydrogen has just one proton. An atom of helium, the gas put in party balloons to make them float, has two protons and two neutrons. An atom of the heavy metal called lead has 82 protons and 124 neutrons.

▶ The bits inside an atom give each substance its features, from exploding hydrogen to life–giving oxygen.

Hydrogen   Helium   Oxygen

Electron
Proton
Neutron

It is hard to imagine the size of an atom. A grain of sand, smaller than this o, contains at least 100 billion billion atoms. If you could make the atoms bigger, so that each one becomes as big as a pin head, the grain of sand would be 2 kilometres high!

Electron

Nucleus made from protons and neutrons

'Nano' means one-billionth (1/1,000,000,000th), and nanotechnology is science at the smallest level – how atoms join to make molecules. It is fairly new, but it has already produced many useful products, from stronger materials in jet planes and racing cars, to self-cleaning glass and bouncier tennis balls!

Movement of electrons

▲ The protons and neutrons in the nucleus of an atom are held together by a powerful force.

◄ This idea for a nano gear-bearing allows the central axle to spin inside the outer collar. It could be used in micromachines.

▼ Buckyballs are ball-shaped structures made of carbon atoms, used in some types of solar panels and medical research.

► Like buckyballs, nanotubes are formed mainly of carbon atoms. They can be combined with plastics in hi-tech equipment such as racing bicycles.

Science in nature

Science and its effects are found all over the natural world. Scientists study animals, plants, rocks and soil. They want to understand nature, and find out how science and its technology affect wildlife.

One of the most complicated types of science is ecology. Ecologists try to understand how the natural world links together. They study how animals and plants live, what animals eat, and why plants grow better in some soils than others. They count the numbers of animals and plants and may trap animals briefly to study them, or follow the growth of trees in a wood. When the balance of nature is damaged, ecologists can help to find out why.

▼ One of the most important jobs in science is to study damage and pollution in the natural world. Almost everything we do affects wild places and animals and plants. For example, the power station here may make the river water warmer. This could encourage animals and plants accidentally introduced from tropical areas, which change the balance of nature.

▼ The science of ecology involves long periods of studying nature in all kinds of habitats, from rivers to the seabed. For example, observing birds like herons, and fish such as trout, shows which foods they eat. This helps us to understand how changes to the habitat may affect them.

KEY

1. Water beetle
2. Rainbow trout
3. Water scorpion
4. Banded demoiselle damselfly
5. Heron
6. Otter
7. Warbler
8. Power station
9. Reedmace

◀ Oil spills and leaks cause vast damage to a region's ecology. Scientists advise on the best ways to clear up the pollution.

Ecologists use many forms of high-tech science in their studies. They may fit an animal with a radio-collar so that its movements can be tracked. Special cameras see in the dark and show how night hunters catch their prey. Radar used to detect planes can also follow flocks of birds. The sonar (echo-sounding) equipment of boats can track shoals of fish or whales.

◀ Tracking tigers is vital to know the threats faced by these endangered big cats, and help to save them.

Body science

One of the biggest areas of science is medicine. Medical scientists work to produce better drugs, more spare parts for the body and more machines for use by doctors. They also carry out scientific research to find out how people can stay healthy and prevent disease.

▲ Medical technology uses the latest equipment to diagnose illness, treat life-threatening conditions and cure diseases. This monitoring unit displays heart rate, pulse rate, amounts of oxygen in the blood, breathing speed, blood pressure and other vital signs.

As parts of the body work, such as the muscles and nerves, they produce tiny pulses of electricity. Pads on the skin pick up these pulses, which are displayed as a wavy line on a screen or paper strip. The ECG (electro-cardiograph) machine shows the heart beating. The EEG (electro-encephalograph) shows nerve signals flashing around the brain.

Laser beam hits retina inside eye

▶ A laser beam shines safely through the front of the eye to mend inner problems such as a detached retina.

Laser beams are ideal for delicate operations, or surgery, on body parts such as the eye. The beam makes very small, precise cuts. It can be shone into the eye and made most focused, or strongest, inside. So it can make a cut deep within the eye, without any harm to the outer parts.

▶ An endoscope is inserted into the body to give a doctor a picture on screen. The treatment can be given immediately.

MAKE A PULSE MACHINE

You will need:
modelling clay   drinking straw

Find your pulse by feeling your wrist, just below the base of your thumb, with a finger of the other hand. Place some modelling clay on this area, and stick a drinking straw into it. Watch the straw twitch with each heartbeat. Now you can see and feel your pulse. Check your pulse rate by counting the number of heartbeats in one minute.

The endoscope is like a flexible telescope made of fibre-strands. This is pushed into a body opening such as the mouth, or through a small cut, to see inside. The surgeon looks into the other end of the endoscope, or at a picture on a screen.

Endoscope tube

Image from endoscope

Water supply

Science in the future

Many modern machines and processes can cause damage to our environment and our health. The damage includes acid rain, destruction of the ozone layer and the greenhouse effect, leading to climate change and global warming. Science can help to find solutions. New filters and chemicals called catalysts can reduce dangerous fumes from vehicle exhausts and power stations, and in the chemicals in factory waste pipes.

Fumes from power station cause acid rain

Oil storage tanks bring risk of leaks

◄ Fumes, waste and chemicals cause terrible pollution in many cities.

Intensive farming ruins soil

Ships may spill oil or fuel

QUIZ

If you become a scientist, which science would you like to study? See if you can guess what these sciences are:

1. Meteorology   2. Biology
3. Astronomy   4. Ecology

Bottles crushed

Crushed glass
into furnace

Bottle bank for
empty glassware

Molten glass
poured into
moulds

Bottles cool
and glass
hardens

Bottles filled
and used

▶ Sorting waste
into different
materials such as
glass, plastic and
cardboard before it
is collected makes
recycling much more
efficient.

WE
RECYCLE

▲ Recycling glass saves enormous
amounts of energy and raw materials.

One very important area of
science is recycling. Many
materials and substances can be
recycled – glass, paper, plastics,
cans, scrap metals and rags.
Scientists are working to improve
the process. Products should be
designed so that when they no
longer work, they are easy to
recycle. The recycling process itself
is also being made more effective.

We use vast amounts of energy, especially
to make electricity and as fuel in our cars.
Much of this energy comes from crude oil
(petroleum), natural gas and coal. But these
energy sources will not last for ever. They also
cause huge amounts of pollution. Scientists are
working to develop cleaner forms of energy,
which will produce less pollution and not run out.
These include wind power from turbines, solar
power from photocells, and hydroelectric and
tidal power from dams.

Rotor blade

Spinner

Pylon

▶ In a wind turbine, the
mechanical spinning movement
from the rotor is changed into
electrical energy.

INVENTIONS

Humans have always been inventors. More than one million years ago, our ancient relatives made simple stone tools. Around 30,000 years ago our more recent ancestors were much more skilled at tool-making (1) and they had worked out how to sew skins together to make clothes (2). The first musical instruments were made from bone more than 20,000 years ago (3). Early humans lived by hunting animals, and invented bows and arrows to which they added tips of sharp stone. Tools, clothes, weapons, dwellings and other inventions gradually became more complicated and numerous.

▶ Stone Age clothes were made out of animal skins sewn together using a bone needle.

The first inventions

The first inventors lived about 2.5 million years ago. They were small, human-like creatures who walked upright on two legs. Their first inventions were stone tools. They hammered stones with other stones to shape them. These rough tools have been found in Tanzania in Africa. Scientists call this early relative of ours 'handy man'.

Spear made from wood with tip of sharp flint

Stone Age people made really sharp weapons and tools by chipping a stone called flint. They dug pits and tunnels in chalky ground to find the valuable flint lumps. Their digging tools were made from reindeer antlers.

▲ Flint tools were shaped to fit comfortably into the hand, with finely chipped cutting edges that could cut through large bones.

Early hunters were able to kill the largest animals. With flint tips on their weapons, they overcame wild oxen and horses and even killed huge, woolly mammoths. They used their sharp flint tools to carve up the bodies. The flint easily sliced through tough animal hides.

▼ Stone Age hunters trapped woolly mammoths in pits and killed them with spears and stones.

Stone

Pit covered with sticks

The axe was a powerful weapon. A new invention, the axe handle, made it possible to strike very hard blows. Fitted with a sharp stone head, the axe was useful for chopping down trees for firewood and building shelters.

▶ Axe heads were valuable, and were traded with people who had no flint.

MODERN AXE

▶ A modern axe is made of steel but it still has a long, sharp cutting edge and wooden handle.

▶ Saws were made from about 12,000 BC, and had flint 'teeth' held in place by resin.

MODERN SAW

▲ Today's steel saws also use many small sharp teeth to slice tough materials.

I DON'T BELIEVE IT!

Some Stone Age hunters used boomerangs! They made them out of mammoth tusks thousands of years before Australian boomerangs, and used them for hunting.

Saws could cut through the hardest wood. Flint workers discovered how to make very small flint flakes. They fixed the flakes like teeth in a straight handle of wood or bone. If the teeth broke, they could add new ones. Saws were used to cut through tough bones as well as wood.

Making fire

People once used fire created by lightning. The first fire-makers probably lived in East Asia more than 400,000 years ago. As modern humans spread from Africa, over 60,000 years ago, they found that northern winters were very cold, and fire helped them stay warm. They discovered how to twirl a fire stick very fast – by placing the loop of a bowstring around the stick and moving the bow back and forth. After thousands of years, people invented a way to make sparks from steel by hitting it with a flint. Now they could carry their fire-making tinderboxes around with them.

▲ People discovered that very hot flames would harden, or 'fire', pottery in oven–like kilns.

▶ Fire provided early people with warmth, light and heat to cook food. The temperature deep within a cave stays the same whatever the weather outside.

MAKING HEAT

When your hands are cold you rub them together. Do this slowly. They feel the same. Now rub them together really fast. Feel how your hands get warmer. Rubbing things together is called friction. Friction causes heat.

Fire makes food taste good. The invention of cooking made food safer, because cooking kills germs. Cooking roots and meat on a fire makes them more tender as well as tastier. Humans are the only animals that cook food.

▲ Some people like cooking outdoors on a fire, as our relatives did over a quarter of a million years ago.

Humans invented lamps to light deep, dark caves. The lamps were saucers of clay or stone that burned animal fat, with moss for a wick. Campfire flames kept wild animals away at night. They also cooked food and kept people warm. People could see to make wall paintings in the caves.

New ways of moving

With wheels you can move huge weights. Once, heavy weights were dragged along the ground, sometimes on sledges – parts of 7000-year-old sledges have been found in Scandinavia. Then, more than 5500 years ago, the Sumerians of Mesopotamia began to make wheels from carved planks, which they fastened together.

Metal rim

Plank fastening

▲ Plank wheels were very heavy, and metal rims helped hold them together.

Warriors had light, strong wheels on their fighting chariots. Wheels with spokes are lighter than solid plank wheels. From about 1800 BC, the ancient Egyptians were using light chariots with spoked wheels. Horses pulled them fast in battle. The ancient Greeks and Romans used them for chariot races as well as for fighting.

Lightweight frame

Light rim

Spoke

◀ Spoked wheels made chariots light, fast and easy to steer.

1818
Hobby

1861
Velocipede (Boneshaker)

Early 1870s
Penny Farthing

1976   Mountain bike

▲ Bicycle design has come a long way – early designs were very heavy, and had no pedals or way of steering.

Railway lines were once made of wood! Wheels move easily along rails. Horses pulled heavy wagons on these wagonways over 400 years ago. William Jessop invented specially shaped metal wheels to run along metal rails in 1789. Modern trains haul enormous loads at great speed along metal rails.

▲ The first public railway opened in 1825 and was 40 kilometres long. A century later, steam trains like this puffed across whole continents.

In 1861, bikes with solid tyres were called boneshakers! An even earlier version of the bicycle was sometimes called the 'hobby horse'. It had no pedals, so riders had to push their feet against the ground to make it move. The invention of air-filled rubber tyres made cycling more comfortable.

QUIZ

Which came first?

1. (a) the chariot, or
   (b) the sledge?
2. (a) solid wheels, or
   (b) spoked wheels?
3. (a) rails, or
   (b) steam engines?

Answers:
1.b 2.a 3.a

▼ Wheels this size are usually only found on giant dump trucks. These carry heavy loads such as rocks or soil that can be tipped out.

Cars with gigantic wheels can drive over other cars! Big wheels give a smooth ride. At some motor shows, trucks with enormous wheels compete to drive over rows of cars. Tractors with huge wheels were invented to drive over very rough ground.

On the farm

The first farmers used digging sticks. In the area now called Iraq, about 9000 BC, farmers planted seeds of wheat and barley. They used knives made of flint flakes fixed in a bone or wooden handle to cut the ripe grain stalks. The quern was invented to grind grain into flour between two stones.

▲ Curved knives made of bone or wood were used for harvesting grain.

▼ Ploughed furrows made it easier to sow, water and harvest crops.

Humans pulled the first ploughs. They were invented in Egypt and surrounding countries as early as 4000 BC. Ploughs broke the ground and turned over the soil faster and better than digging sticks. Later on, oxen and other animals pulled ploughs. The invention of metal ploughs made ploughing much easier.

I DON'T BELIEVE IT!

Some Stone Age people invented the first fridges! They buried spare food in pits dug in ground that was always frozen.

For thousands of years, farming hardly changed. Then from about 300 years ago a series of inventions made it much more efficient. One of these was a seed-drill, invented by Englishman Jethro Tull. Pulled by a horse, it sowed seeds at regular spaces in neat rows. It was less wasteful than the old method of throwing grain onto the ground.

Side seed-box

Main seed-box

Coulter bar

▲ Jethro Tull's seed-drill sowed three rows of seed at a time.

Modern machines harvest huge fields of wheat and other crops in record time. The combine harvester was invented to cut the crop and separate grain at the same time. Teams of combine harvesters roll across the plains of America, Russia, Australia and many other places, harvesting the wheat. What were once huge areas of land covered with natural grasses now provide grain for bread.

Scientists are changing the way plants grow. They have invented ways of creating crop plants with built-in protection from pests and diseases. Other bumper crop plants grow well in places where once they could not grow at all because of the soil or weather.

▼ The latest combine harvesters have air-conditioned, soundproofed cabs and nearly all have sound systems. Some even use satellite navigation (satnav or GPS receivers) to plot their route automatically around fields.

From stone to metal

Sometimes pieces of pure natural gold or copper can be found in the ground. The first people to work metal lived in the eastern Mediterranean around 8000 BC, and beat these metals with stone tools. They made the first copper weapons and gold ornaments.

▲ Gold is quite a soft metal. Early goldsmiths beat it into a variety of shapes and made patterns of hammered indentations on its surface to create beautiful objects.

▶ Bronze axe heads were sharper, and less easily damaged, than stone ones.

Blowing air onto flames makes them hotter. About 8500 years ago people discovered how to melt metals out of the rocks, or ores, containing them. They invented bellows – animal-skin bags, to blow air onto the flames. The hot flames melted the metal out of the ore. We call this 'smelting' the metal.

Bronze weapons stay sharper for longer than copper ones. About 5500 years ago, metal workers invented bronze by smelting copper ores and tin ores together. They used the bronze to make hard, sharp swords, spearheads and axe heads.

Bellows

Heat source

Molten bronze

Stone mould

◀ Molten bronze was poured into moulds of stone or clay to make tools.

▲ After smelting, iron was beaten into shape to make strong, sharp weapons.

▲ Iron chains are made by hammering closed the red-hot links.

Armies with iron weapons can beat armies with bronze weapons. Iron is harder than bronze, but needs a very hot fire to smelt it. About 1500 BC, metal workers began to use charcoal in their fires. This burns much hotter than ordinary wood and is good for smelting iron.

The Romans were excellent plumbers. They made water pipes out of lead instead of wood or pottery. Lead is soft, easily shaped and is not damaged by water.

▼ At a smelting works metal ore is heated past its melting point and the liquid is poured to set in a mould.

Some modern steelworks are the size of towns. Steel is made from iron, and was first invented when small amounts of carbon were mixed into molten iron. Steel is very hard, and used to build many things, including ships and skyscrapers.

► Burj Khalifa in Dubai is the world's tallest building, at 829.8 metres. It has a steel framework weighing more than 4000 tonnes.

Boats and sails

Viking explorers reached America 1000 years ago. The world's first boats were log rafts, useful for carrying heavy loads, but very slow. Viking boats were fast, and could travel far across the open sea. Sails were invented at least 5000 years ago, and the Vikings used both sails and oars.

▶ Viking boats were made of long planks fitted onto wooden frames, and steered by means of a long oar fastened near the stern (back of the ship). They could be sailed across deep oceans, or rowed up shallow rivers, and made river journeys from the Baltic as far as the Black Sea.

I DON'T BELIEVE IT!

In 450 BC a merchant called Himilco sailed from North Africa to Britain. He ended up in Cornwall and bought Cornish tin!

About 300 years ago sailing ships sailed all the world's oceans. Some, like the British man-of-war fighting ships, were enormous, with many sails and large crews of sailors. Countries such as Britain, France, Spain and Holland had large navies made up of these ships.

Some sailing boats race around the world non-stop. Modern sailing boats use many inventions, such as machines to roll up the sails and gears that allow the boat to steer itself. These boats are tough, light and very fast.

▲ Sailing ships called caravels, designed in the 1400s, were light, easily steered and ideal for exploring. Early ones had lanteen (triangular) sails, with square ones added later.

▶ Modern ocean-going yachts have a huge balloon-like sail called a spinnaker, invented in the mid-1800s. It is used mainly when heading in the direction the wind is blowing.

Sailing into the unKnown

Early sailors looked at the stars to find their way about. Around 1000 BC, Phoenician merchants from Syria were able to sail out of sight of land without getting lost. They knew in which direction certain stars lay. The north Pole Star, in the Little Bear constellation (star group), always appears in the north.

▲ Two stars in the Great Bear constellation are called the Pointers. They point to the north Pole Star in the Little Bear constellation.

Magnetic compasses always point north and south. They allow sailors to navigate (find their way) even when the stars are invisible. The Chinese invented the magnetic compass about 3000 years ago. It was first used in Europe about 1000 years ago.

◄ Compasses have a magnetized needle placed on a pivot so it can turn easily. Beneath this is a card with marked points to show direction.

Early maps showed where sea monsters lived. The first attempt at a world map was drawn by the Greek Ptolemy in AD 160. Greek maps of around 550 BC showed the known world surrounded by water in which monsters lived. Over 500 years ago, Pacific islanders had maps of sticks and shells, showing islands and currents. The first globe was invented in 1492 by a German, Martin Behaim.

▶ Using stick and shell maps, Pacific islanders successfully crossed thousands of kilometres of ocean.

Shell = island
Stick = current
Reed binding

Mirrors

Telescope

Moving arm

▼ The chronometer was invented by Englishman John Harrison in 1735. It was a reliable timepiece, specially mounted to remove the effect of a ship's motion at sea.

Frame

▶ The sextant was developed around 1730 and was an important navigation aid until the 1900s.

Scale

Eighteenth-century sailors could work out exactly where they were on the oceans. They used an instrument called a sextant, invented around 1730. The sextant measured the height of the Sun from the horizon. The chronometer was an extremely reliable clock that wasn't affected by the motion of the sea.

USING A COMPASS

Take a compass outside and find out which direction is north. Put a cardboard arrow with 'N' on it on the ground pointing in the right direction. Then try to work out the directions of south, west and east.

▼ Modern navigation instruments use signals from several satellites to pinpoint their position.

Antenna (aerial) detects signals from available satellites

Batteries

Receiver compares the available satellite signals and 'locks on' to the three strongest ones

Display screen

New direction-finding inventions can tell anyone exactly where they are. A hand-held instrument, called a GPS receiver, receives signals from satellites in space. It shows your position to within a few metres. These receivers can be built into cars, ships, planes – even mobile phones!

Weapons of war

▶ Medieval sieges of well-protected forts or cities sometimes lasted for months.

Trebuchet

Siege tower

Battering ram

Ballista

The Romans invented massive rock-hurling weapons. In medieval times, armies in Europe and the Middle East still used the same weapons in city and castle sieges. The trebuchet slung great rocks or burning material over city walls. The ballista fired missiles such as stones or spears with huge force at the enemy.

The first gunpowder was used in fireworks. The Chinese invented gunpowder over 1000 years ago. In 1221 they used it to make exploding bombs and in 1282 they invented the first gun, a cannon. Cannons and mortars, which fired bombs or large stone balls very high through the air, were used in European sieges from the 14th century onwards. The first small firearms carried by soldiers appeared in the 15th century.

The battering ram could smash through massive city walls and gates. The Egyptians may have invented it in 2000 BC to destroy brick walls. It was a huge tree-trunk, often with an iron head, swung back and forth in a frame. Sometimes it had a roof to protect the soldiers from rocks and arrows from above.

Gunpowder was used in tunnels to blow up castle walls. Attackers in a siege dug tunnels under the walls and supported them with wooden props. Then, they blew up or burned away the props so that the walls collapsed.

Greek fire was a secret weapon that burned on water. The Greeks invented it in the 7th century AD to destroy ships attacking Constantinople. A chemical mixture was squirted at enemies through copper pipes. It was still being used many centuries later in medieval sieges, pumped down onto the heads of attackers.

▼ The biggest battleship guns can hurl explosive shells more than 40 kilometres.

▲ The Gatling gun could fire six bullets a second.

Modern machine guns can fire thousands of bullets per minute. Richard Gatling, an American, invented a gun that would later lead to the development of the machine gun in 1862. As in all modern guns, each machine-gun bullet has its own metal case packed with deadly explosives.

Measuring time

The huge stone slabs of Stonehenge can be used as a calendar. Some of its stones are lined up with sunrise on the longest day of the year. It was built and rebuilt in Wiltshire in southern England between 3000 and 1550 BC.

Pointer

Hour markings

Shadow

1862 - 1867

▶ A sundial's shadow moves from west to east during the day.

▼ Raising the huge main stones of Stonehenge required the muscles of many workers and the know-how of skilled Bronze Age engineers.

One of the earliest clocks was a stick stuck in the ground. Invented in Egypt up to 4000 years ago, the length and position of the shadow gave the time of day. Later sundials had a face with hours, and a pointer that cast a shadow.

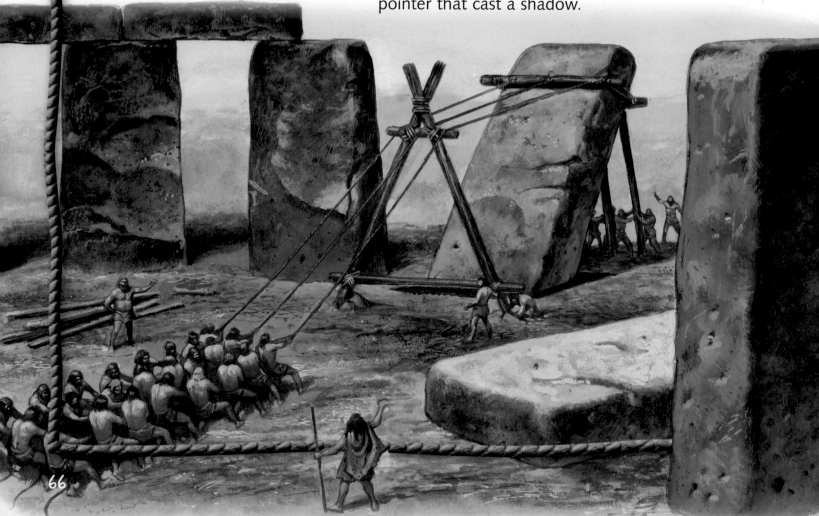

Candles, water and sand can all be used to tell the time. The Egyptians invented a clock that dripped water at a fixed rate about 1400 BC. Candle clocks were marked with rings, and in the hourglass, invented about AD 1300, sand ran between two glass globes.

▶ An hourglass shows a time period has passed, not the time of day.

◀ Until the invention of quartz movements, wristwatches contained springs and cogs.

Gear wheel

Ratchet wheel

You can't see any moving parts in a modern quartz clock. Early clocks depended on movement. A Dutchman, Christiaan Huygens, invented a clock in 1656 which depended on a swinging pendulum. About the same time, clocks driven by coiled springs were invented. Modern quartz crystal clocks work on invisible vibrations and are very accurate. They were first produced in 1929.

Some clocks are like toys. Swiss cuckoo clocks contain a bird on a spring that flies out of a little door and 'cuckoos' the time. Some 18th-century clocks looked like ships, and their guns fired to mark the hours.

▶ Wristwatches were not made until 1790. Many modern watches have a liquid crystal display (LCD) and show changing numerals instead of hour and minute hands.

MAKE A SHADOW CLOCK

Fix about 60 centimetres of garden cane upright in a flat piece of ground. Use lollipop sticks or twigs to mark the length and position of the shadow every hour, from 9 a.m. to 4 p.m., if possible. Which hour casts the shortest shadow?

Harvesting nature's energy

The first inventions to use wind power were sailing boats. Invented around 3500 BC by the Egyptians, and also by the Sumerians of Mesopotamia, the first sailing boats had a single square sail. By AD 600, windmills for grinding grain had been invented in Arab countries. Some European windmills, in use from about AD 1100 onwards, could be turned to face the wind.

The first waterwheels invented were flat, not upright. The ancient Greeks were using upright wheels more than 2100 years ago, and the Romans improved the design with bucket-like containers and gears to slow the turning rate. As well as grinding corn, some were used to drive pumps or saws.

Sail

Direction vane

Main drive

Rotation point

Vertical shaft

Gears

Millstones

Flour chute

▶ Many windmills were made entirely of wood apart from the millstones.

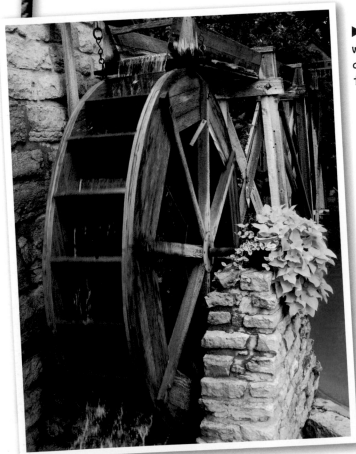

◀ In overshot watermills, the water strikes the top of the millwheel.

▲ Hydroelectric dams change the energy of moving water into electrical energy.

Early steam engines often threatened to explode. Thomas Savery's 1698 steam pump, invented in Devon, England, wasted fuel and was dangerous. Englishman Richard Trevithick developed a steam engine to move on tracks in 1804.

Generator changes the spinning movement from the rotor into electrical energy

The angle of the blades changes according to the speed of the wind

Spinning magnets can create an electric current. Michael Faraday and other scientists invented the first magnetic electricity generators (producers) in the 1830s. Today, huge dams use the power of millions of tonnes of flowing water to turn electricity generators, which have spinning electromagnets inside them.

Yaw control pod swings around to keep the rotor blades pointing into the wind

The strength of the wind usually increases the higher up you are. Some of the largest wind turbines in use today stand as high as a 50-storey building, with propellers spanning more than the length of a football pitch. They produce enough electricity to power 5000 homes or more.

▶ An increasing number of wind turbines are being built to make electricity.

Rotor blade

Marks on a page

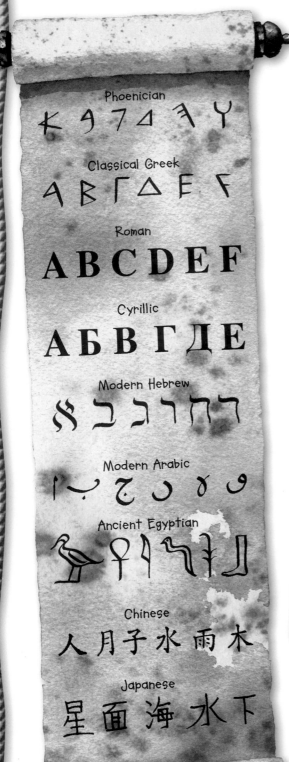

Phoenician

K 𝟦 𝟟 𝚫 ⫪ 𐤘

Classical Greek

𝚲 Ꭺ Ᏼ Γ Δ E Ϝ

Roman

ABCDEF

Cyrillic

АБВГДЕ

Modern Hebrew

ה ד ג ב א

Modern Arabic

Ancient Egyptian

Chinese

人 月 子 水 雨 木

Japanese

星 面 海 水 下

▲ Ancient picture writing used hundreds of different signs, but most modern alphabets have far fewer letters.

The first writing was made up of pictures. Writing was invented by the Sumerians 5500 years ago. They scratched their writing onto clay tablets. The most famous word pictures are the 'hieroglyphs' of ancient Egyptians from about 5000 years ago. Cuneiform writing was made up of wedge shapes pressed into clay with a reed. It followed the Sumerian picture writing.

▲ Some of the religious books handwritten by monks were decorated with beautiful illustrations.

The world's earliest books were rolls of paper made from reeds. The first of this kind was produced in Egypt between 1500 BC and 1350 BC and was called 'The Book of the Dead'. Christian monks used to write their religious books on sheets of parchment made from animal skins.

◀▲ Early printing presses were made of wood, and used movable wooden letters.

Reading suddenly became much more popular after the invention of printing. A German, Johannes Gutenberg, was an early inventor of a printing press with movable letters in the 15th century. By the end of the century there were printing presses all over Europe.

Once, people were expert at doing sums on their fingers. The first written numbers were invented about 3100 BC by Middle Eastern traders. Around AD 300, the Chinese invented a counting machine called an abacus. It was a frame with beads strung on wires. Some people still use them.

Container of ink is punched open to release the ink, and pressurized to get the ink into the nozzle area

▼ Modern home printers build up the image as many tiny dots of ink forming a long row or line, and then another line next to it, and so on.

Print head zooms to and fro along a guide rail, squirting out tiny jets of ink

New sheets of paper are fed from the paper tray through a tiny gap by rubber rollers

Printed sheets pile up in the print tray

Power button

▼ Experts can do complicated sums very fast on an abacus.

Computers do sums at lightning speed. Early modern computers were invented in the United States and Europe in the 1930s and 1940s. Today, computers are small, cheap and extremely powerful. They can store whole libraries of information. The Internet allows everyone to share information and send messages immediately almost anywhere in the world.

I DON'T BELIEVE IT!

Some early Greek writing was called, 'the way an ox ploughs the ground'. It was written from right to left, then the next line went left to right, and so on, back and forth.

Making things bigger

Small pieces of glass can make everything look bigger. Spectacle-makers in Italy in the 14th century made their own glass lenses to look through. These helped people to read small writing. Scientists later used these lenses to invent microscopes, to see very small things, and telescopes, to see things that are far away.

▲ Spectacles became important as more people began to read books.

Scientists saw the tiny bacteria that cause illness for the first time with microscopes. The Dutch invented the first microscopes, which had one lens. In the 1590s Zacharias Janssen of Holland invented the first microscope with two lenses, which was much more powerful.

◄ Early microscopes with two or more lenses, like those of English inventor Robert Hooke (1635–1703), were powerful, but the image was unclear.

The Dutch tried to keep the first telescope a secret. Hans Lippershey invented it in 1608, but news soon got out. Galileo, an Italian scientist, built one in 1609. He used it to get a close look at the Moon and the planets.

QUIZ

1. Which came first, (a) the telescope, or (b) spectacles?
2. Do you study stars with (a) a microscope, or (b) a telescope?
3. Which are smaller, (a) bacteria, or (b) ants

Answers:
1.b 2.b 3.a

Modern microscopes make things look thousands of times bigger. A German, Ernst Ruska, invented the first electron microscope in 1933. It made things look 12,000 times their actual size. The latest microscopes can magnify things millions of times.

◀ An electron microscope shows a tiny parasite in monstrous detail, but this tick is actually less than 15 millimetres long.

You cannot look through a radio telescope. An American, Grote Reber, invented the first one and built it in his backyard in 1937. Radio telescopes pick up radio signals from space with a dish-shaped receiver. The signals come from distant stars, and, more recently, from space probes.

▶ Most radio telescope dishes can be moved to face in any direction.

Making music

Humans are the only animals that play tunes on musical instruments. Stone Age people made rattles and similar noise-makers from mammoth bones and tusks. Instruments you hit or rattle are called percussion instruments, and are still used in modern orchestras.

▼ The instruments of the modern orchestra are grouped into sections according to type – usually string, woodwind, brass and percussion.

GUIDE TO THE ORCHESTRA

- **Percussion** instruments, such as drums, produce sound when they are made to vibrate by being hit, rubbed, shaken or scraped.
- **Brass** instruments, such as horns, are made of curled brass tubes. Sound is produced by blowing into a cup-shaped mouthpiece.
- **Woodwind** instruments produce sound when a player blows against an edge (as in flutes) or through a wooden reed (as in clarinets).
- **String** instruments have strings. They produce sound when their strings are plucked or bowed.

Over 20,000 years ago Stone Age Europeans invented whistles and flutes. They made them out of bones or antlers. Modern flutes still work in a similar way – the player covers and uncovers holes in a tube while blowing across it.

The earliest harps were made from tortoise shells. They were played in Sumeria and Egypt about 5000 years ago. Modern harps, similar to most ancient harps, have strings of different lengths.

Percussion

Trumpets

Horns

Clarinets

Piccolo and Flutes

Violas

Harp

2nd violins

1st violins

Conductor

Pianos have padded hammers inside, which strike the strings. The first piano-like instrument was invented in about 1480 and its strings were plucked, not struck, when the keys were pressed. It made a softer sound than a modern piano.

▲ The grand piano's strings are laid out horizontally in a harp-shaped frame.

Timpani

Trombones

Tubas

Bassoons

Oboes

Double basses

Cellos

The trumpet is among the loudest instruments in the orchestra. A trumpet-like instrument was found in Tutankhamen's tomb in Egypt dating back to 1320 BC. Over 2000 years ago, Celtic warriors in northern Europe blew bronze trumpets shaped like mammoth tusks to frighten their enemies.

◄ The trumpet, played here by award-winning Alison Balsom, has a total tubing length of about 148 centimetres as well as three moveable valves.

Bagpipes sound as strange as they look. They were invented in India over 2000 years ago. The Roman army had bagpipe players. In the Middle Ages, European and Middle Eastern herdsmen sometimes played bagpipes while they looked after their animals.

▶ Some modern bagpipes still have a bag of sewn animal skins.

Keeping in touch

Some African tribes used to use 'talking drums' to send messages. Native Americans used smoke signals, visible several miles away. Before electrical inventions such as the telephone, sending long-distance messages had to be a simple process.

Wooden arms on tall poles across the country sent signals hundreds of miles in 18th-century France. Claude Chappe invented this system, now called semaphore, in 1797. Until recently, navies used semaphore flags to signal from ship to ship. In 1838 American Samuel Morse invented a code of short and long bursts of electric current or light, called dots and dashes. It could send messages along a wire, or could be flashed with a light.

◀ Skilled morse code operators could send 30 words per minute.

▼ Each position of the semaphore signaller's arms forms a different letter. What does this message say?

S   I   G

N   A   L

The telephone can send your voice around the world. A Scotsman, Alexander Graham Bell, invented it in the 1870s. When you speak, your voice is changed into electric signals that are sent along to a receiver held by the other user. Within 15 years there were 140,000 telephone owners in the United States.

Transmitter   Receiver

J.T.B. DEL.

▶ Bell's early telephone (top) in 1876 had one of the first electrical loudspeakers. The modern moving-coil design was invented in 1898 by Oliver Lodge.

▼ Smartphones have a touch-sensitive screen rather than buttons or keys.

Protective screen

Touch screen

Power button

Metal case

Small but powerful and long-lasting rechargeable battery

Sockets link the phone physically to a computer or network, to download or upload information

▼ The mobile network is divided into areas called 'cells', each with a receiver-transmitter mast, linked by combinations of wires, radio waves, microwaves, optical fibres and satellites.

Uplink to telecom satellite

Downlink to hub

Main hub

Person makes a call on cellphone A

Radio link to local mast

Person receives the call on cellphone B

With a mobile or cellphone you can talk to practically anyone wherever you are. Your voice is carried on radio waves or microwaves and passed from antenna to antenna until it reaches the phone you are calling. Some of the antennas are on space satellites.

Radio signals fly through the air without wires. An Italian, Guglielmo Marconi, invented the radio or 'wireless' in 1899. Radio stations send signals, carried on invisible radio waves, which are received by an antenna. A Scot, John Logie Baird, invented an early TV system in 1926. TV pictures can travel through the air or along wires.

I DON'T BELIEVE IT!

Early TV performers had to wear thick, clown-like makeup. The pictures were so fuzzy that viewers could not make out their faces otherwise.

► Live TV images can be beamed to a satellite in space, then redirected to the other side of the world.

Taking to the skies

The first hot-air balloon passengers were a sheep, a duck and a cockerel. The French Montgolfier brothers invented the hot-air balloon in 1782. The first human passengers often had to put out fires, as the balloon was inflated by hot air created by burning straw and wool!

▲ The Montgolfier hot-air balloon made the first untethered, manned flight from Paris in 1783.

► The Wright Flyer had a spruce wood frame and canvas covering. It flew with the small wing at the front.

Many inventors have tried to fly by flapping bird-like wings. All have failed. One of the first bird-men crashed to his death at a Roman festival in the 1st century AD.

The first aircraft flight lasted just 12 seconds. The Wright brothers invented their airplane and flew it in 1903 in the United States. In 1909 a Frenchman, Louis Blériot, flew across the Channel. In World War I (1914–1918), airplanes were used in combat. In World War II (1939–1945), aircraft such as the British Spitfire beat off German air attacks.

► Da Vinci's helicopter used an 'air screw' popular in toys.

▼ Formed in 1965, the Royal Air Force Aerobatic Team, known as the Red Arrows, uses Hawk jets. They need perfect timing to perform their close formation flying and aerobatics at high speed.

Englishman Frank Whittle invented the first jet engine in 1930. Most modern aircraft are jets without propellers. Teams of jets, such as the Red Arrows, often perform stunts at air shows. In 1947 American Chuck Yeager flew faster than the speed of sound in the rocket plane Bell X–1.

The first model helicopter was made by Leonardo da Vinci as long ago as 1480. In 1877, an Italian, Enrico Forlanini, invented a model of a steam helicopter which flew for almost half a minute and reached a height of over 10 metres. Modern helicopters can hover and land almost anywhere, and are often used for rescue missions at land and sea.

I DON'T BELIEVE IT!

In 1783 the first hydrogen balloon was attacked and destroyed by terrified farm workers when it landed. It had flown 24 kilometres.

▲ The Westland Sea King, retired in Britain in 2011, was one of the world's most successful helicopters. It excelled at SAR (Search and Rescue), being able to hover steadily even in stormy winds.

Keeping a record

▼ Thomas Edison produced many important inventions, including sound recording, electric light bulbs and an early film-viewing machine.

The first sound recording was the nursery rhyme, 'Mary had a little lamb'. In 1877 an American, Thomas Edison, invented a way of recording sounds by using a needle to scratch marks on a cylinder or tube. Moving the needle over the marks again repeated the sounds. Performers spoke or sang into a horn, and the sounds were also played back through it.

To play the first disc records, you had to keep turning a handle. Emile Berliner, a German, invented disc recording in 1887. The discs were played with steel needles, and soon wore out. They also broke easily if you dropped them. Long-playing discs appeared in 1948. They had 20 minutes of sound on each side and were made of bendy plastic, which didn't break so easily.

MODERN MUSIC PLAYER

▲ Digital music players can hold over two weeks of sound recording, played through earphones or a dock with speakers.

▼ Early record players had to be wound up between records, and the loudspeaker was a large horn.

QUIZ

1. Were the first recordings on (a) discs, or (b) cylinders?
2. Which came first, (a) movies, or (b) long-playing records?
3. Was the first photograph of (a) flowers, or (b) rooftops?
4. The first movies were viewed through a hole in a box – true or false?

Answers:
1.b 2.a 3.b 4.True

It took eight hours to take the world's first photograph in 1826. Frenchman Joseph Nicéphore Niépce was the inventor, and the first photograph was of rooftops. Early cameras were huge, and the photos were on glass plates. In 1881 Peter Houston invented rolls of film, which George Eastman developed for the company Kodak, making photography much easier.

▲ Digital cameras have a display screen that shows the view the lens sees, which is the image that will be stored.

▲ The Lumière brothers, who invented the movie projector, also made films and opened the first public cinema.

Only one person at a time could watch the first movies. The viewer peered through a hole in a box. Thomas Edison's company invented movies in 1888. The invention of a projector in 1895 by the French Lumière brothers allowed a whole audience to watch the film on a screen.

▶ Launched in 2001, the iPod took little more than one year to develop.

The forerunner of the MP3 player was the portable laser-based CD player. It was more than ten times bigger and heavier than an iPod. Moving it often made the compact disc (CD) skip.

Round the house

A horse and cart were needed to move the first successful vacuum cleaner around. An English engineer, Hubert Cecil Booth, invented it in 1902. The first 'Hoover' electric vacuum cleaner was built from a wooden box, an electric fan and an old sack in 1907 in America.

▼ Refrigerators were once large, noisy and had little food space.

▲ Early vacuum cleaners worked by opening and closing a bellows with a handle.

Early refrigerators, invented in the 19th century, killed many people. They leaked the poisonous gas that was used to cool them. In 1929 the gas was changed to a non-poisonous one called freon. We now know that freon causes damage to the planet's atmosphere, so that has been changed too.

A melted chocolate bar led to the invention of the microwave oven. An American, Percy L. Spencer, invented it in 1953 after noticing that a microwave machine where he worked had melted the chocolate in his pocket. In a microwave oven the microwaves make the food heat itself up from the inside.

▲ In a microwave oven the microwaves are deflected by metal vanes down onto the food below.

There is no air inside a light bulb. If there was, it would burn out in no time. The first light bulbs failed because air could get in. American Thomas Edison invented an air-tight light bulb in 1879 that could burn for a long time. He opened the first electric light company in 1882.

Vacuum bulb

Filament

◀ In a light bulb, electricity causes a wire filament to glow brightly in the airless bulb.

▲ Energy-saving bulbs make light using fluorescence, where a chemical substance called phosphor lining the tube glows.

Screw thread

Power contact

Four thousand years ago in Crete in Greece the king's palaces had flushing toilets. They used rainwater. In England, toilets that flushed when you pulled a handle were invented in the 18th century. In 1885 Thomas Twyford invented the first all-china flushing toilet.

From Earth into space

Concorde flew at twice the speed of sound, nearly 2150 kilometres an hour. This is at least twice as fast as the earliest jets. The huge jet airliner crossed the Atlantic at a height of over 18,000 metres. All Concordes were retired in 2003.

◀ The Chinese were the first to use gunpowder in war, as in this hand-held gun for firing missiles.

Rockets helped the Chinese drive away a Mongol army in the 13th century. The rockets used gunpowder, which the Chinese had invented 300 years earlier, but had only used in fireworks.

German war rockets in World War II (1939–1945) could travel 320 kilometres to hit England. They were invented by a scientist called Wernher von Braun. After the war he helped the United States build space rockets.

▼ German rocket pioneer von Braun designed the Saturn V rockets that launched the Apollo astronauts to the Moon. Here he shows an early version to US President Eisenhower.

I DON'T BELIEVE IT!

A 15th-century Chinaman, Wan Hu, tried to make a flying machine out of 47 rockets and two kites. His servants lit all the rockets at the same time, and Wan Hu disappeared forever in a massive explosion.

The Apollo 11 spacecraft landed the first men on the Moon in 1969. On Earth people watched on TV as Neil Armstrong and Buzz Aldrin stepped down onto the Moon's surface.

The Space Shuttle travelled on a giant fuel tank with side rockets into space. Then the tank and rockets dropped away and the shuttle circled the Earth at a height of 241 kilometres. American scientists invented the reusable Space Shuttle, which first flew in 1981. The shuttles were retired in 2011.

◄ The Space Shuttle used rockets to enter space, but came back without them, landing on a runway like a giant glider.

Command module

Lunar module

Separation point

Separation point

3rd stage one J-2 engine

2nd stage containing fuel

Separation point

Engines

1st stage containing fuel

1st stage five J-2 engines

USA

▲ The three-stage Saturn V rocket carried the spacecraft of the first men to land on the Moon. It weighed over 2700 tonnes.

▼ The mighty Saturn V's forerunner was a tiny liquid-fuelled rocket, invented by Robert Goddard in 1926.

USA

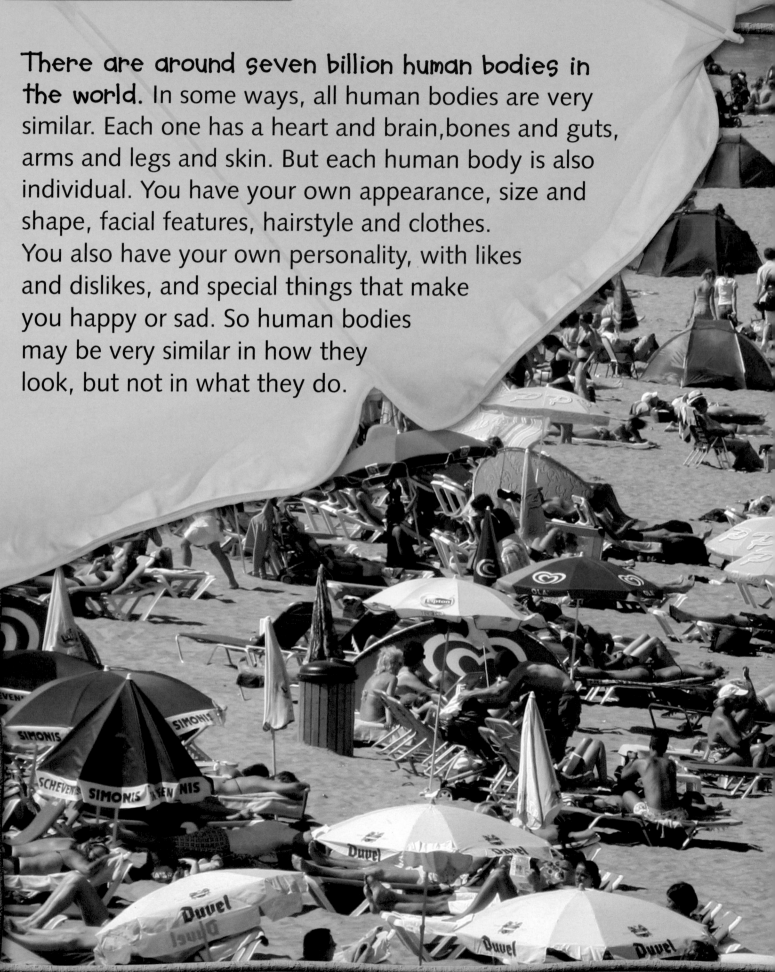

HUMAN BODY

There are around seven billion human bodies in the world. In some ways, all human bodies are very similar. Each one has a heart and brain, bones and guts, arms and legs and skin. But each human body is also individual. You have your own appearance, size and shape, facial features, hairstyle and clothes. You also have your own personality, with likes and dislikes, and special things that make you happy or sad. So human bodies may be very similar in how they look, but not in what they do.

▲ We tend to notice small differences on the outside of human bodies, such as height, width, hair colour and clothes. This allows us to recognize our family and friends.

Baby body

Successful sperm

Egg cell

A full-grown human body is made of billions of microscopic parts, called cells. But in the beginning, the body is a single cell, smaller than this full stop. Yet it contains all the instructions, known as genes, for the whole body to grow and develop.

Wall of uterus

Fluid around baby

Bones of skeleton start to form

Hair begins to grow on head

Placenta (afterbirth)

Two months

Face has taken shape

Three months

▲►Thousands of sperm cells reach the egg (top), but only one is successful and joins with it, at fertilization. This starts the growth of the baby, shown here after two, three, five, seven and nine months.

Baby begins to move and kick

Five months

Umbilical cord

Seven months

The body begins when an egg cell inside the mother joins up with sperm from the father. The egg cell splits into two cells, then into four cells, then eight, and so on. The bundle of cells embeds itself in the mother's womb (uterus), which protects and nourishes it. Soon there are thousands of cells, then millions, forming a tiny embryo. After two months the embryo has grown into a tiny baby, as big as your thumb, with arms, legs, eyes, ears and a mouth.

Wall of womb is stretched

Umbilical cord

Placenta

Baby is born head-first

Nine months

Cervix (neck of womb)

After nine months in the womb, the baby is ready to be born. Strong muscles in the walls of the womb tighten, or contract. They push the baby through the opening, or neck of the womb, called the cervix, and along the birth canal. The baby enters the outside world.

A newborn baby may be frightened and usually starts to cry. Inside the womb it was warm, wet, dark, quiet and cramped. Outside there are lights, noises, voices, fresh air and room to stretch. The crying is also helpful to start the baby breathing, using its own lungs.

Being born can take an hour or two – or a whole day or two. It is very tiring for both the baby and its mother. After birth, the baby starts to feel hungry and it feeds on its mother's milk. Finally, mother and baby settle down for a rest and some sleep.

▲ Once the baby is settled it is time for its mother to admire her newborn and rest.

89

The growing body

A new baby just seems to eat, sleep and cry. It feeds on milk when hungry and sleeps when tired. Also, it cries when it is too hot, too cold, or when its nappy needs changing.

A new baby is not totally helpless. It can do simple actions called reflexes, to help it survive. If something touches the baby's cheek, it turns its head to that side and tries to suck. If the baby hears a loud noise, it opens its eyes wide, throws out its arms and cries for help. If something touches the baby's hand and fingers, it grasps tightly.

A new baby looks, listens, touches and quickly learns. Gradually it starts to recognize voices, faces and places. After about six weeks, it begins to smile. Inside the body, the baby's brain is learning very quickly. The baby soon knows that if it laughs, people will laugh back and if it cries, someone will come to look after it.

WHAT HAPPENS WHEN?

Most babies learn to do certain actions in the same order. The order is mixed up here. Can you put it right?

walk, crawl, roll over, sit up, smile, stand

Answers:
smile, roll over, sit up, crawl, stand, walk

▼ In the grasping reflex, the baby tightly holds anything that touches its hand or fingers. Its grip is surprisingly strong!

▼ Most babies crawl before they walk, but some go straight from sitting or 'bottom-shuffling' to walking.

As a baby grows into a child, at around 18 months, it learns ten new words every day, from 'cat' and 'dog' to 'sun' and 'moon'. There are new games such as piling up bricks, new actions such as throwing and kicking, and new skills such as using a spoon at mealtimes and scribbling on paper.

At about three months old, most babies can reach out to hold something, and roll over when lying down. By the age of six months, most babies can sit up and hold food in their fingers. At nine months, many babies are crawling well and perhaps standing up. By their first birthday, many babies are learning to walk and starting to talk.

At the age of five, when most children start school, they continue to learn an amazing amount. This includes thinking or mental skills such as counting and reading, and precise movements such as writing and drawing. They learn out of the classroom too – how to play with friends and share.

▼ Playing is lots of fun, but it's learning too, as children develop control over the muscles in their fast-growing bodies.

91

On the body's outside

Skin's surface is made of tiny cells that have filled up with a hard, tough substance called keratin, and then died. So when you look at a human body, most of what you see is 'dead'! The cells get rubbed off as you move, have a wash and get dry.

Skin rubs off all the time, and grows all the time too. Just under the surface, living cells make more new cells that gradually fill with keratin, die and move up to the surface. It takes about four weeks from a new skin cell being made to when it reaches the surface and is rubbed off. This upper layer of skin is called the epidermis.

Hair

Oil gland

Epidermis

Dermis

▲ This view shows skin magnified (enlarged) about 50 times.

Hair follicle

▲ Lots of dead skin is removed without you realizing when you dry yourself after a shower.

Skin's lower layer, the dermis, is thicker than the epidermis. It is made of tiny, bendy, thread-like fibres of the substance collagen. The dermis also contains small blood vessels, tiny sweat glands, and micro-sensors that detect touch.

One of skin's important jobs is to protect the body. It stops the delicate inner parts from being rubbed, knocked or scraped. Skin also prevents body fluids from leaking away and it keeps out dirt and germs.

SENSITIVE SKIN

You will need:

a friend   sticky-tack
two used matchsticks   ruler

1. Press some sticky-tack on the end of the ruler. Press two matchsticks into the sticky-tack, standing upright, about 1 centimetre apart.

2. Make your friend look away. Touch the back of their hand with both matchstick ends. Ask your friend: 'Is that one matchstick or two?' Sensitive skin can detect both ends

3. Try this at several places, such as on the finger, wrist, forearm, neck and cheek.

Safety helmet protects head and brain

Elbow-pads cushion fall

Gloves save fingers from scrapes and breaks

Knee-pads prevent hard bumps

▲ Skin is tough, but it sometimes needs help to protect the body. Otherwise it, and the body parts beneath, may get damaged.

Skin helps to keep the body at the same temperature. If you become too hot, sweat oozes onto your skin and, as it dries, draws heat from the body. Also, the blood vessels in the lower layer of skin widen, to lose more heat through the skin. This is why a hot person looks sweaty and red in the face.

Skin gives us our sense of touch. Millions of microscopic sensors in the lower layer of skin, the dermis, are joined by nerves to the brain. These sensors detect different kinds of touch, from a light stroke to heavy pressure, heat or cold, and movement. Pain sensors detect when skin is damaged. Ouch!

Hair and nails

There are about 120,000 hairs on the head, called scalp hairs. There are also eyebrow hairs and eyelash hairs. Grown-ups have hairs in the armpits and between the legs, and men have hairs on the face. And everyone, even a baby, has tiny hairs all over the body – 5 to 10 million of them!

Blonde wavy hair is the result of carotene from an oval hair follicle

Black curly hair is the result of black melanin from a flat hair follicle

Straight red hair is the result of red melanin from a round hair follicle

◄ Hair contains pigments (coloured substances) – mainly melanin (dark brown) and some carotene (yellowish). Different amounts of pigments, and the way their tiny particles are spread out, cause different hair colours.

Each hair grows from a deep pit in the skin, called a follicle. The hair is only alive where it gets longer, at its base or root, in the bottom of the follicle. The rest of the hair, called the shaft, is like the surface of the skin – hard, tough, dead and made of keratin. Hair helps to protect the body, especially where it is thicker and longer on the head. It also helps to keep the body warm in cold conditions.

Straight black hair is the result of black melanin from a round follicle

Scalp hairs get longer by about 3 millimetres each week, on average. Eyebrow hairs grow more slowly. No hairs live forever. Each one grows for a time, then it falls out, and its follicle has a 'rest' before a new hair sprouts. This is happening all the time, so the body always has some hairs on each part.

Nails, like hairs, grow at their base (the nail root) and are made of keratin. Also like hairs, nails grow faster in summer than in winter, and faster at night than by day. Nails lengthen by about half a millimetre, on average, each week.

Nail root

Cuticle (skin edge)

Nail bed

Bone inside finger

▲ The growing nail root is hidden under skin. The nail slides slowly along the nail bed.

▲ Nails make the fingertips stronger and more rigid for pressing hard on guitar strings. Slightly longer nails pluck the strings.

Nails have many uses, from peeling off sticky labels to plucking guitar strings or scratching an itch. They protect and stiffen the ends of the fingers, where there are nerves that give us our sense of touch.

I DON'T BELIEVE IT!

A scalp hair grows for up to five years before it falls out and gets replaced. Left uncut during this time, it would be about one metre long. But some people have unusual hair that grows faster and for longer. Each hair can reach more than 5 metres in length before dropping out.

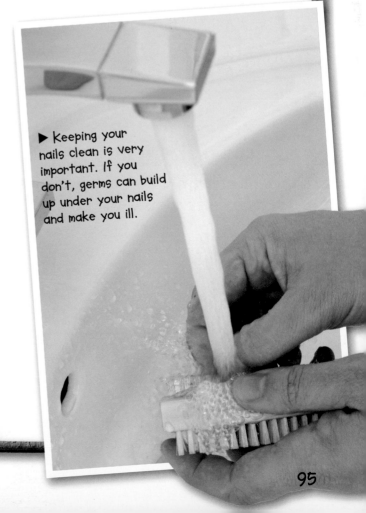

▶ Keeping your nails clean is very important. If you don't, germs can build up under your nails and make you ill.

The bony body

Without bones, the body would be as floppy as a jellyfish! Bones do many jobs. The long bones in the arms work like levers to reach out the hands. The finger bones grasp and grip. Bones protect softer body parts. The dome-like skull protects the brain. The ribs shield the lungs and heart. Bones also produce blood cells, as explained on the opposite page.

Cranium (skull)

Mandible (lower jaw)

Sternum (breastbone)

Clavicle (collarbone)

Rib

Humerus

Vertebra (backbone)

Ulna

Radius

Pelvis (hip bone)

Femur (thigh bone)

Patella (kneecap)

Tibia

Fibula

Heel bone

Toe bone

Suture

◀ The skull has deep bowls for the eyes, and small holes where nerves pass through to join the brain inside.

▶ The skeleton forms a strong framework inside the body. The only artificial (man-made) substances that can match bone for strength and lightness are some of the materials used to make racing cars and jet planes.

All the bones together make up the skeleton. Most people have 206 bones, from head to toe as follows:
- 8 in the upper part of the skull, the cranium or braincase
- 14 in the face
- 6 tiny ear bones, 3 deep in each ear
- 1 in the neck, which is floating and not directly connected to any other bone
- 26 in the spinal column or backbone
- 25 in the chest, being 24 ribs and the breastbone
- 32 in each arm, from shoulder to fingertips (8 in each wrist)
- 31 in each leg, from hip to toetips (7 in each ankle)

Bone contains threads of the tough, slightly bendy substance called collagen. It also has hard minerals such as calcium and phosphate. Together, the collagen and minerals make a bone strong and rigid, yet able to bend slightly under stress. Bones have blood vessels for nourishment and nerves to feel pressure and pain. Also, some bones are not solid. They contain a jelly-like substance called marrow. This makes tiny parts for the blood, called red and white blood cells.

Nerves and blood vessels

Marrow

Spongy bone

Compact (hard) bone

'Skin' of bone (periosteum)

End or head of bone

▲ Bone has a hard layer outside, a spongy layer next, and soft marrow in the middle.

NAME THE BONE!
Every bone has a scientific or medical name, and many have ordinary names too. Can you match up these ordinary and scientific names for various bones?

1. Mandible 2. Femur 3. Clavicle 4. Pelvis 5. Patella 6. Sternum

a. Thigh bone b. Breastbone c. Kneecap d. Hip bone e. Collarbone f. Lower jaw bone

Answers:
1f 2a 3e 4d 5c 6b

The flexible body

Without joints, almost the only parts of your body that could move would be your tongue and eyebrows! Joints between bones allow the skeleton to bend. You have more than 200 joints. The largest are in the hips and knees. The smallest are in the fingers, toes, and between the tiny bones inside each ear which help you hear.

▼ This X-ray shows a dislocated (out of place) shoulder. The shoulder joint has the biggest range of movement, so this injury is common.

There are several kinds of joints, depending on the shapes of the bone ends, and how much the bones can move. Bend your knee and your lower leg moves forwards and backwards, but not sideways. This is a hinge-type joint. Bend your hip and your leg can move forwards, backwards, and also from side to side. This is a ball-and-socket joint.

Shoulder blade

Collarbone

Head of upper arm bone

TEST YOUR JOINTS

Try using these different joints carefully, and see how much movement they allow. Can you guess the type of joint used in each one — hinge or ball-and-socket?

1. Fingertip joint (smallest knuckle)
2. Elbow
3. Hip
4. Shoulder

Answers:
1. hinge 2. hinge
3. ball-and-socket 4. ball-and-socket

Inside a joint where the bones come together, each bone end is covered with a smooth, shiny, slippery, slightly springy substance, known as cartilage. This is smeared with a thick liquid called synovial fluid. The fluid works like the oil in a car, to smooth the movements and reduce rubbing and wear between the cartilage surfaces.

The bones in a joint are linked together by a bag-like part, the capsule, and strong, stretchy, strap-like ligaments. The ligaments let the bones move but stop them coming apart or moving too far. The shoulder has seven strong ligaments.

In some joints, there are cartilage coverings over the bone ends and also pads of cartilage between the cartilage! These extra pads are called articular discs. There is one in each joint in the backbone, between the spinal bones, which are called vertebrae. There are also two of these extra cartilages, known as menisci, in each knee joint. They help the knee to 'lock' straight so that we can stand up without too much effort.

Muscle

Patella (kneecap)

Femur

Tendon

Ligament

Cartilage pad

Fibula

Tibia

▲ The knee has many ligaments, cartilage pads (menisci) and strong tendons that anchor muscles.

KEY
① Swivel joint
② Ellipsoidal joints
③ Saddle joint
④ Ball-and-socket joint
⑤ Hinge joint
⑥ Plane joints

◄ Synovial joints allow the body to move in many ways so we can walk, run, play and work.

When muscles pull

Almost half the body's weight is muscles, and there are more than 640 of them! Muscles have one simple but important job, which is to get shorter, or contract. A muscle cannot forcefully get longer.

▼ A tendon is stuck firmly into the bone it pulls, with a joint stronger than superglue!

Pectoralis

Biceps

Deltoid

Abdominal wall muscles

Trapezius

Rectus femoris

Tendon

Gluteus

Bone

Semitendinosus

Gastrocnemius

▲ The muscles shown here are those just beneath the skin, called superficial muscles. Under them is another layer, the deep muscle layer. In some areas there is an additional layer, the medial muscles.

A muscle is joined to a bone by its tendon. This is where the end of the muscle becomes slimmer or tapers, and is strengthened by strong, thick fibres of collagen. The fibres are fixed firmly into the surface of the bone.

Some muscles are wide or broad, and shaped more like flat sheets or triangles. These include the three layers of muscles in the lower front and sides of the body, called the abdominal wall muscles. If you tense or contract them, they pull your tummy in to make you look thinner.

Most muscles are long and slim, and joined to bones at each end. As they contract they pull on the bones and move them. As this happens, the muscle becomes wider, or more bulging in the middle. To move the bone back again, a muscle on the other side of it contracts, while the first muscle relaxes and is pulled longer.

I DON'T BELIEVE IT!

It's easier to smile than to frown. There are about 40 muscles under the skin of the face. You use almost all of these to make a deep frown, but only about half of them to show a broad grin.

Every muscle in the body has a scientific or medical name, which is often quite long and complicated. Some of these names are familiar to people who do exercise and sports. The 'pecs' are the pectoralis major muscles across the chest. The 'biceps' are the biceps brachii muscles in the upper arms, which bulge when you bend your elbow.

▶ A breakdancer needs endurance, strength and control over their muscles to carry out moves such as this.

If you take plenty of exercise or play sport, you do not gain new muscles. But the muscles you have become larger and stronger. This keeps them fit and healthy. Muscles which are not used much may become weak and floppy.

Biceps gets shorter and bends the elbow

To move the forearm back down, the triceps shortens and the biceps gets longer

▶ Muscles work in two-way pairs, like the biceps and triceps, which bend and straighten the elbow.

Biceps — Triceps

Muscles have many shapes and sizes, but inside they are all similar. They have bundles of long, hair-like threads called muscle fibres, or myofibres. Each muscle fibre is slightly thinner than a hair. A big muscle has many thousands of them. Most are about 3 or 4 centimetres long. In a big muscle, many fibres of different lengths lie alongside each other and end-to-end.

Muscle fibre

Nerve branches

Muscle fibre

Muscle fibril

▶ Male gymnasts need extreme upper body strength when using the rings. Many different muscles work together to hold the gymnast in the correct position.

Each muscle fibre is made of dozens or hundreds of even thinner parts, called muscle fibrils or myofibrils. There are millions of these in a large muscle. And, as you may guess, each fibril contains hundreds of yet thinner threads! There are two kinds, actin and myosin. As the actins slide past and between the myosins, the threads get shorter – and the muscle contracts.

Body of muscle

◀ The main part of a muscle is the body or belly, with hundreds of muscle fibres inside.

Actin

Myosin

▶ Dozens of arm and hand muscles move a pen precisely, a tiny amount each time.

Muscles are controlled by the brain, which sends messages to them along string-like nerves. When a muscle contracts for a long time, its fibres 'take turns'. Some of them shorten powerfully while others relax, then the contracted ones relax while others shorten, and so on.

The body's biggest muscles are the ones you sit on – the gluteus maximus muscles in the buttocks. The longest muscle is the sartorius, across the front of the thigh. Some of its fibres are more than 30 centimetres in length. The most powerful muscle, for its size, is the masseter in the lower cheek, which closes the jaws when you chew.

WHICH MUSCLES?

Can you match the names of these muscles with different parts of the body?

a. Gluteus maximus b. Masseter
c. Sartorius d. Cardiac muscle
e. Pectoralis major

1. Heart 2. Chest 3. Front of thigh
4. Buttock 5. Mouth

Answers:
a4 b5 c3 d1 e2

The breathing body

The body cannot survive more than a few minutes without breathing. This action is so important, we do it all the time without thinking. We breathe to take air into the body. Air contains the gas oxygen, which is needed to get energy from food to power all of the body's vital life processes.

▲ Scuba divers wear special breathing apparatus called 'aqua lungs'. They control their breathing to make their oxygen supply last as long as possible.

► Body parts make up the respiratory system in the head, neck and chest. These carry out the process of breathing air to take oxygen into the body.

Nasal chamber

Nose

Voice-box (larynx)

Windpipe

Bronchus

Left lung

Diaphragm

Parts of the body that work together to carry out a main task are called a system. The parts that carry out breathing are the respiratory system. These parts are the nose, throat, windpipe, the air tubes or bronchi in the chest, and the lungs.

The nose is the entrance for fresh air to the lungs – and the exit for stale air from the lungs. The soft, moist lining inside the nose makes air warmer and damper, which is better for the lungs. Tiny bits of floating dust and germs stick to the lining or the hairs in the nose, making the air cleaner.

▼ When playing the trumpet, the diaphragm and chest control the air flowing in and out of the lungs.

The windpipe, or trachea, is a tube leading from the back of the nose and mouth, down to the lungs. It has about 20 C-shaped hoops of cartilage in its wall to keep it open, like a vacuum cleaner hose. Otherwise the pressure of body parts in the neck and chest would squash it shut.

At the top of the windpipe, making a bulge at the front of the neck, is the voice-box or larynx. It has two stiff flaps, vocal cords, which stick out from its sides. Normally these flaps are apart for easy breathing. But muscles in the voice-box can pull the flaps almost together. As air passes through the narrow slit between them it makes the flaps shake or vibrate – and this is the sound of your voice.

HUMMMMMM!

You will need:

stopwatch

Do you think making sounds with your voice-box uses more air than breathing? Find out by following this experiment.

1. Take a deep breath in, then breathe out at your normal rate, for as long as you can. Time the out-breath.

2. Take a similar deep breath in, then hum as you breathe out, again for as long as you can. Time the hum.

3. Try the same while whispering your favourite song, then again when singing.

▲ The vocal cords are held apart for breathing (top) and pulled together for speech (bottom).

105

Breathing parts

The main parts of the respiratory (breathing) system are the two lungs in the chest. Each one is shaped like a tall cone, with the pointed end at shoulder level.

Air comes in and out of the lungs along the windpipe, which branches at its base to form two main air tubes, the bronchi. One goes to each lung. Inside the lung, each bronchus divides again and again, becoming narrower each time. Finally the air tubes, thinner than hairs, end at groups of tiny 'bubbles' called alveoli.

Left bronchus

Muscles in wall of bronchus

Air space inside bronchus

Right lung

View along inside of bronchus

I DON'T BELIEVE IT!

On average, the air breathed in and out through the night by a sleeping person, would fill an average-sized bedroom. This is why some people like to sleep with the door or window open!

There are more than 200 million tiny air bubbles, or alveoli, in each lung. Inside, oxygen from breathed-in air passes through the very thin linings of the alveoli to equally tiny blood vessels on the other side. The blood carries the oxygen away, around the body. At the same time a waste substance, carbon dioxide, seeps through the blood vessel, into the alveoli. As you breathe out, the lungs blow out the carbon dioxide.

Breathing needs muscle power! The main breathing muscle is the dome-shaped diaphragm at the base of the chest. To breathe in, it becomes flatter, making the lungs bigger, so they suck in air down the windpipe. At the same time, rib muscles lift the ribs, also making the lungs bigger. To breathe out, the diaphragm and rib muscles relax. The stretched lungs spring back to their smaller size and blow out stale air.

Air in   Air out

Diaphragm pulls down   Diaphragm relaxes

▲ Breathing uses two main sets of muscles, the diaphragm and those between the ribs.

▶ After great activity, the body breathes faster and deeper, to replace the oxygen used by the muscles for energy.

Bronchiole

Blood vessel

Air space in alveoli

Alveoli

▲ Inside each lung, the main bronchus divides again and again, into thousands of narrower airways called bronchioles.

As you rest or sleep, each breath sends about half a litre of air in and out, 15 to 20 times each minute. After great activity, such as running a race, you need more oxygen. So you take deeper breaths faster – 3 litres or more of air, 50 times or more each minute.

The hungry body

All machines need fuel to make them go, and the body is like a living machine whose fuel is food. Food gives us energy for our body processes inside, and for breathing, moving, talking and every other action we make. Food also provides raw materials that the body uses to grow, maintain itself and repair daily wear-and-tear.

We would not put the wrong fuel into a car engine, so we should not put unsuitable foods into the body. A healthy diet needs a wide variety of foods, which have lots of vital nutrients. Too much of one single food may be unhealthy, especially if that food is very fatty or greasy. Too much of all foods is also unhealthy, making the body overweight and increasing the risk of illnesses.

► It is important for children to learn how to cook healthily. Grilling or barbecuing food is much healthier than frying it.

▲ Fresh fruits such as bananas, and vegetables such as carrots, have lots of vitamins, minerals and fibre, and are good for the body in lots of ways.

▼ Foods such as bread, pasta and rice contain lots of starch, which is a useful energy source.

There are six main kinds of nutrients in foods, and the body needs balanced amounts of all of them.

- Proteins are needed for growth and repair, and for strong muscles and other parts.
- Carbohydrates, such as sugars and starches, give plenty of energy.
- Some fats are important for general health and energy.
- Vitamins help the body to fight germs and disease.
- Minerals are needed for strong bones and teeth and also healthy blood.
- Fibre is important for good digestion and to prevent certain bowel disorders.

◄ Fish, low-fat meats such as chicken, and dairy produce such as cheese all contain plenty of valuable proteins.

▲ Fats and oily foods are needed in moderate amounts. Plant oils are healthier than fats and oils from animal sources.

FOOD FOR THOUGHT
Which of these meals do you think is healthier?

Meal A
Burger, sausage and lots of chips, followed by ice cream with cream and chocolate.

Meal B
Chicken, tomato and a few chips, followed by fresh fruit salad with apple, banana, pear and melon.

Answer:
Meal B

Bite, chew, gulp

The hardest parts of your whole body are the ones that make holes in your food — teeth. They have a covering of whitish or yellowish enamel, which is stronger than most kinds of rocks! Teeth need to last a lifetime of biting, nibbling, gnashing, munching and chewing. They are your own food processors.

There are four main shapes of teeth. The front ones are incisors, and each has a straight, sharp edge, like a spade or chisel, to cut through food. Next are canines, which are taller and more pointed, used mainly for tearing and pulling. Behind them are premolars and molars, which are lower and flatter with small bumps, for crushing and grinding.

Incisor

Canine

Premolar

Molar

Jaw bone

Root

▲ In an adult, each side (left and right) of each jaw (upper and lower) usually has eight different-shaped teeth, of four main types.

Soft core or pulp

Enamel

Dentine

Jaw bone

Gum

◄ At the centre of a tooth is living pulp, with many blood vessels and nerve endings that pass into the jaw bone.

A tooth may look almost dead, but it is very much alive. Under the enamel is slightly softer dentine. In the middle of the tooth is the dental pulp. This has blood vessels to nourish the whole tooth, and nerves that feel pressure, heat, cold and pain. The lower part of the tooth, strongly fixed in the jaw bone, is the root. The enamel-covered part above the gum is the crown.

Teeth are very strong and tough, but they do need to be cleaned properly and regularly. Germs called bacteria live on old bits of food in the mouth. They make waste products which are acid and eat into the enamel and dentine, causing holes called cavities. Which do you prefer – cleaning your teeth after main meals and before bedtime, or the agony of toothache?

▶ Clean your teeth by brushing in different directions and then flossing between them. They will look better and stay healthier for longer.

▼ The first set of teeth lasts about ten years, while the second set can last ten times longer.

First set
(milk or deciduous teeth)

Second set
(adult or permanent set)

Teeth are designed to last a lifetime. Well, not quite, because the body has two sets. There are 20 small teeth in the first or baby set. The first ones usually appear above the gum by about six months of age, the last ones at three years old. As you and your mouth grow, the baby teeth fall out from about seven years old. They are replaced by 32 larger teeth in the adult set.

After chewing, food is swallowed into the gullet (oesophagus). This pushes the food powerfully down through the chest, past the heart and lungs, into the stomach.

① Tongue pushes food to the back of the throat

② Throat muscles squeeze the food downwards

③ The oesophagus pushes food to the stomach

Food's long journey

The digestive system is like a tunnel about 9 metres long, through the body. It includes parts of the body that bite food, chew it, swallow it, churn it up and break it down with natural juices and acids, take in its goodness, and then get rid of the leftovers.

The stomach is a bag with strong, muscular walls. It stretches as it fills with food and drink, and its lining makes powerful digestive acids and juices called enzymes, to attack the food. The muscles in its walls squirm and squeeze to mix the food and juices.

The stomach digests food for a few hours into a thick mush, which oozes into the small intestine. This is only 4 centimetres wide, but more than 5 metres long. It takes nutrients and useful substances through its lining, into the body.

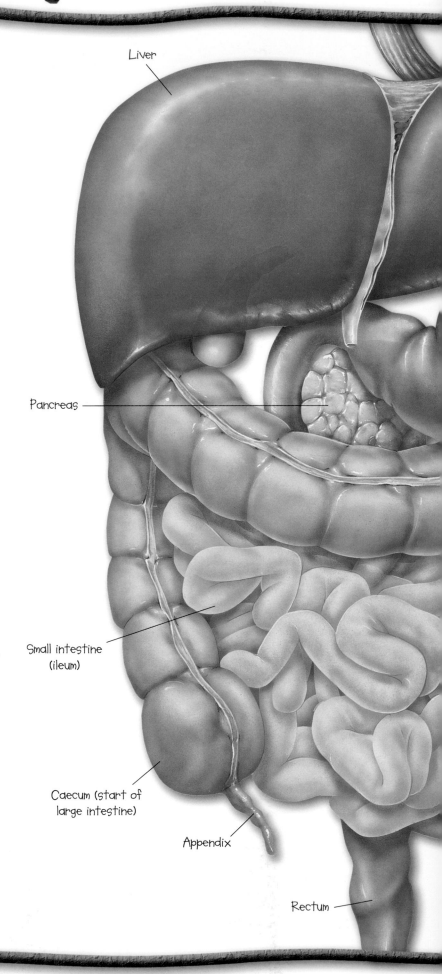

Liver

Pancreas

Small intestine (ileum)

Caecum (start of large intestine)

Appendix

Rectum

The large intestine follows the small one, and it is certainly wider, at about 6 centimetres, but much shorter, only 1.5 metres. It takes in fluids and a few more nutrients from the food, and then squashes what's left into brown lumps, ready to leave the body.

Stomach

Villus

Large intestine

Vessels inside villus

Vessels in intestine lining

▶ The lining of the small intestine has thousands of tiny finger-like parts called the villi, which take nutrients from food, into the blood and lymph system.

◀ The digestive parts almost fill the lower part of the main body, called the abdomen.

The liver and pancreas are also parts of the digestive system. The liver sorts out and changes the many nutrients from digestion, and stores some of them. The pancreas makes powerful digestive juices that pass to the small intestine to work on the food there.

I DON'T BELIEVE IT!

What's in the leftovers? The brown lumps called bowel motions or faeces are only about one-half undigested or leftover food. Some of the rest is rubbed-off parts of the stomach and intestine lining. The rest is millions of 'friendly' but dead microbes (bacteria) from the intestine. They help to digest our food for us, and in return we give them a warm, food-filled place to live.

The heart beats to pump the blood all around the body and pass its vital oxygen and nutrients to every part. The same blood goes round and round, or circulates, in its network of blood vessels. So the heart, blood vessels and blood are known as the circulatory system.

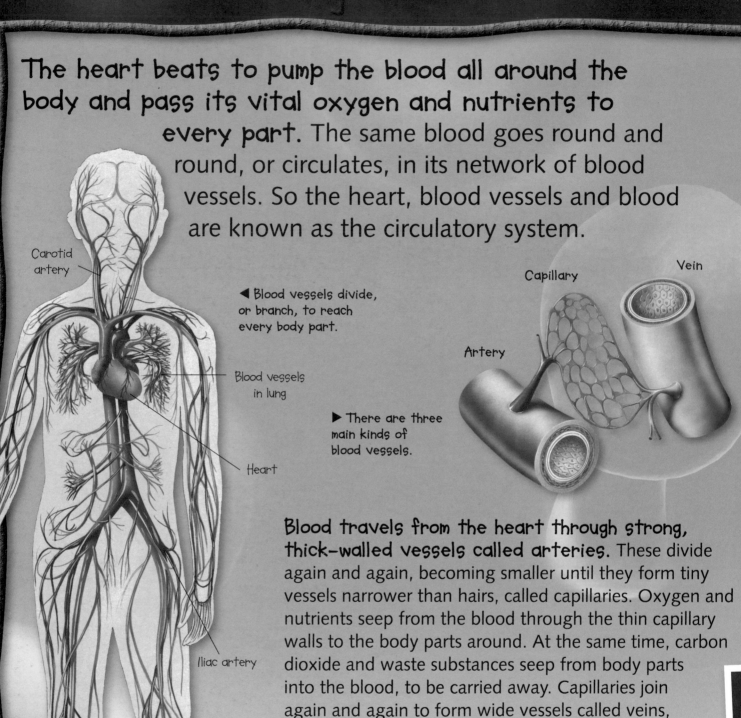

Carotid artery

◀ Blood vessels divide, or branch, to reach every body part.

Blood vessels in lung

Heart

▶ There are three main kinds of blood vessels.

Capillary

Vein

Artery

Iliac artery

Blood travels from the heart through strong, thick-walled vessels called arteries. These divide again and again, becoming smaller until they form tiny vessels narrower than hairs, called capillaries. Oxygen and nutrients seep from the blood through the thin capillary walls to the body parts around. At the same time, carbon dioxide and waste substances seep from body parts into the blood, to be carried away. Capillaries join again and again to form wide vessels called veins, which take blood back to the heart.

In addition to delivering oxygen and nutrients, and carrying away carbon dioxide and wastes, blood has many other vital tasks. It carries body control substances called hormones. It spreads heat evenly around the body from busy, warmer parts such as the heart, liver and muscles. It forms a sticky clot to seal a cut. It carries many substances that attack germs and other tiny invaders.

Blood has four main parts. The largest is billions of tiny, saucer-shaped red cells, which make up almost half of the total volume of blood and carry oxygen. Second is the white cells, which clean the blood, prevent disease and fight germs. The third part is billions of tiny platelets, which help blood to clot. Fourth is watery plasma, in which the other parts float.

QUIZ

Can you match these blood parts and vessels with their descriptions?
a. Artery b. Vein c. White blood cell
d. Red blood cell e. Platelet f. Capillary

1. Large vessel that takes blood back to the heart
2. Tiny vessel allowing oxygen and nutrients to leave blood
3. Large vessel carrying blood away from the heart
4. Oxygen-carrying part of the blood
5. Disease-fighting part of the blood
6. Part that helps blood to clot

Answers:
a3 b1 c5 d4 e6 f2

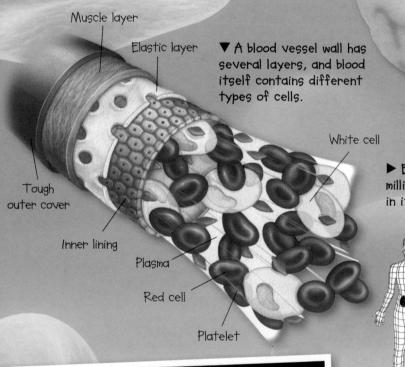

▼ A blood vessel wall has several layers, and blood itself contains different types of cells.

Muscle layer
Elastic layer
Tough outer cover
Inner lining
Plasma
Red cell
Platelet
White cell

▶ Each kidney has about one million tiny filters, called nephrons, in its outer layer, or cortex.

Cortex
Medulla
Blood vessels
Ureter

Blood is cleaned by two kidneys, situated in the middle of your back. They filter the blood and make a liquid called urine, which contains unwanted and waste substances, plus excess or 'spare' water. The urine trickles from each kidney down a tube, the ureter, into a stretchy bag, the bladder. It's stored here until you can get rid of it – at your convenience.

A Positive

AS-1 RED BLOOD CELLS

◀ Blood donation is vital and saves many lives every year.

The beating body

The heart is about as big as its owner's clenched fist. It is a hollow bag of very strong muscle, called cardiac muscle or myocardium. This muscle never tires. It contracts once every second or more often, all through life. The contraction, or heartbeat, squeezes blood inside the heart out into the arteries. As the heart relaxes it fills again with blood from the veins.

Inside, the heart is not one bag-like pump, but two pumps side by side. The left pump sends blood all around the body, from head to toe, to deliver its oxygen (systemic circulation). The blood comes back to the right pump and is sent to the lungs, to collect more oxygen (pulmonary circulation). The blood returns to the left pump and starts the whole journey again.

From upper body

To upper body

Aorta (main artery)

Pulmonary artery to lung

To lung

From lung

Right atrium

Valve

Right ventricle

From lower body

To lower body

▶ The heart is two pumps side by side, and each pump has two chambers, the upper atrium and the lower ventricle.

116

Inside the heart are four sets of bendy flaps called valves. These open to let blood flow the right way. If the blood tries to move the wrong way, it pushes the flaps together and the valve closes. Valves make sure the blood flows the correct way, rather than sloshing to and fro, in and out of the heart, with each beat.

► This X-ray of a chest shows a pacemaker that has been implanted to control an irregular heartbeat.

▲ Doctors use ECG machines to monitor the electrical activity of the heart.

The heart is the body's most active part, and it needs plenty of energy brought by the blood. The blood flows through small vessels, which branch across its surface and down into its thick walls. These are called the coronary vessels.

The heart beats at different rates, depending on what the body is doing. When the muscles are active they need more energy and oxygen, brought by the blood. So the heart beats faster, 120 times each minute or more. At rest, the heart slows to 60 to 80 beats per minute.

HOW FAST IS YOUR HEARTBEAT?

You will need:
plastic funnel   tracing paper
plastic tube (like hosepipe)   sticky-tape
You can hear your heart and count its beats with a sound-funnel device called a stethoscope.
1. Stretch the tracing paper over the funnel's wide end and tape in place. Push a short length of tube over the funnel's narrow end.
2. Place the funnel's wide end over your heart, on your chest, just to the left, and put the tube end to your ear. Listen to and count your heartbeat.

Looking and listening

The body finds out about the world around it by its senses – and the main sense is eyesight. The eyes detect the brightness, colours and patterns of light rays, and change these into patterns of nerve signals that they send to the brain. More than half of the knowledge, information and memories stored in the brain come into the body through the eyes.

▼ The eye is moved by six tiny muscles, and inside, it is filled with a clear fluid, vitreous humour.

Eye muscle

Tear gland

Iris

Pupil

Tear duct to nose

Optic nerve

Choroid

Retina

Lens

Lens muscle

▼ In the retina are wider cone cells, narrower rod cells, and many nerve cells with long fibres connecting them.

Each eye is a ball about 2.5 centimetres across. At the front is a clear dome, the cornea, which lets light through a small, dark-looking hole just behind it, the pupil. The light then passes through a pea-shaped lens, which bends the rays so they shine a clear picture onto the inside back of the eye, the retina. This has 125 million tiny cells, rods and cones, which detect the light and make nerve signals to send along the optic nerve to the brain.

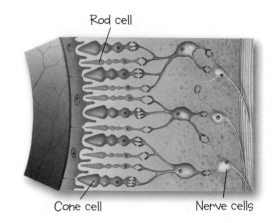

Rod cell

Cone cell

Nerve cells

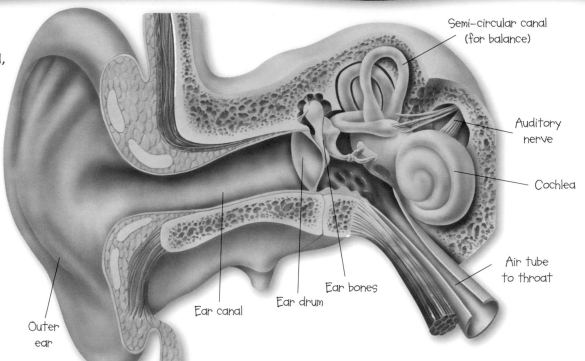

▶ Most of the small, delicate parts of the ear are inside the head, well protected by skull bones around them.

Semi-circular canal (for balance)

Auditory nerve

Cochlea

Air tube to throat

Ear bones

Ear drum

Ear canal

Outer ear

▼ Some people need help to hear properly. A hearing aid worn inside the ear can help them to hear better.

Inside the cochlea, the vibrations pass through fluid and shake rows of thousands of tiny hairs that grow from specialized hair cells. As the hairs vibrate, the hair cells make nerve signals, which flash along the auditory nerve to the brain.

The ear flap funnels sound waves along a short tunnel, the ear canal to the eardrum. As sound waves hit the eardrum it shakes or vibrates, and passes the vibrations to a row of three tiny bones. These are the ear ossicles, the smallest bones in the body. They also vibrate and pass on the vibrations to another part, the cochlea.

BRIGHT AND DIM

Look at your eyes in a mirror. See how the dark hole which lets in light, the pupil, is quite small. The coloured part around the pupil, the iris, is a ring of muscle.

Close your eyes for a minute, then open them and look carefully. Does the pupil quickly get smaller?

While the eyes were closed, the iris made the pupil bigger, to try and let in more light, so you could try to see in the darkness. As you open your eyes, the iris makes the pupil smaller again, to prevent too much light from dazzling you.

Smelling and tasting

▼ The parts that carry out smelling are in the roof of the large chamber inside the nose.

Olfactory cells

Mucus lining

Nasal cavity

You cannot see smells, which are tiny particles floating in the air – but your nose can smell them. Your nose can detect more than 10,000 different scents, odours and fragrances. Smell is useful because it warns us if food is bad or rotten, and perhaps dangerous to eat. That's why we sniff a new or strange food item before trying it.

Smell particles drift with breathed-in air into the nose and through the nasal chamber behind it. At the top of the chamber are two patches of lining, each about the area of a thumbnail and with 5 million olfactory cells. The particles land on their sticky hairs, and if they fit into landing sites called receptors there, like a key into a lock, then nerve signals flash along the olfactory nerve to the brain.

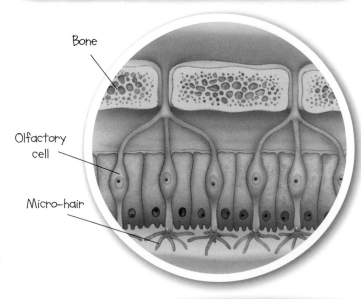

Bone

Olfactory cell

Micro-hair

▶ Olfactory (smell) cells have micro-hairs facing down into the nasal chamber, which detect smell particles landing on them.

The body's most flexible muscle is also the one which is coated with 10,000 micro-sensors for taste — the tongue. Each micro-sensor is a taste bud shaped like a tiny onion. Most taste buds are along the tip, sides and rear upper surface of the tongue. They are scattered around the much larger flaps and lumps on the tongue, which are called papillae.

◄ The tongue is sensitive to flavours, texture and temperature.

Taste works in a similar way to smell, but it detects flavour particles in foods and drinks. The particles touch tiny hairs sticking up from hair cells in the taste buds. If the particles fit into receptors there, then the hair cell makes nerve signals, which go along the facial and other nerves to the brain.

SWEET AND SOUR

The tongue detects four basic flavours.

Which of these foods is sweet, salty, bitter or sour?

1. Coffee 2. Lemon 3. Bacon
4. Ice cream

Answers:
1. bitter 2. sour 3. salty 4. sweet

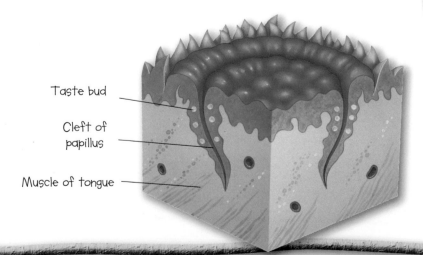

Taste bud

Cleft of papillus

Muscle of tongue

◄ The large pimple-like lumps at the back of the tongue, called papillae, have tiny taste buds in their deep clefts.

The nervous body

Brain

Spinal cord

The body is not quite a 'bag of nerves', but it does contain thousands of kilometres of these pale, shiny threads. Nerves carry tiny electrical pulses known as nerve signals or neural messages. They form a vast information-sending network that reaches every part, almost like the body's own Internet.

Each nerve is a bundle of much thinner parts called nerve fibres. Like wires in a telephone cable, these carry their own tiny electrical nerve signals. A typical nerve signal has a strength of 0.1 volts (one-fifteenth as strong as a torch battery). The slowest nerve signals travel about half a metre each second, the fastest at more than 100 metres per second.

Sciatic nerve

Tibial nerve

Axon

◀ Nerves branch from the brain and spinal cord to every body part.

Dendrites

Synapse (junction between nerve cells)

All nerve signals are similar, but there are two main kinds, depending on where they are going. Sensory nerve signals travel from the sensory parts (eyes, ears, nose, tongue and skin) to the brain. Motor nerve signals travel from the brain out to the muscles, to make the body move about.

▶ The brain and nerves are made of billions of specialized cells, nerve cells or neurons. Each has many tiny branches, dendrites, to collect nerve messages, and a longer, thicker branch, the axon or fibre, to pass on the messages.

Hormones are part of the body's inner control system. A hormone is a chemical made by a gland. It travels in the blood and affects other body parts, for example, making them work faster or release more of their product.

▶ Sports such as snowboarding cause us to produce more adrenaline due to excitement and fear.

The main hormonal gland, the pituitary, is also the smallest. Just under the brain, it has close links with the nervous system. It mainly controls other hormonal glands. One is the thyroid in the neck, which affects the body's growth and how fast its chemical processes work. The pancreas controls how the body uses energy by its hormone, insulin. The adrenal glands are involved in the body's balance of water, minerals and salts, and how we react to stress and fear.

Nerve cell body

Tip of axon

Covering of axon (myelin sheath)

◀ Female and male bodies have much the same hormone-making glands, except for the reproductive parts – ovaries in the female (left) and testes in the male (right).

TIME TO REACT!
You will need:
friend   ruler
1. Ask a friend to hold a ruler by the highest measurement so it hangs down. Put your thumb and fingers level with the other end, ready to grab.
2. When your friend lets go grasp it and measure where your thumb is on the ruler. Swap places so your friend has a go.
3. The person who grabs the ruler nearest its lower end has the fastest reactions. To grab the ruler, nerve signals travel from the eye, to the brain, and back to the muscles in the arm and hand.

The brainy body

Your brain is as big as your two fists side by side. It's the place where you think, learn, work out problems, remember, feel happy and sad, wonder, worry, have ideas, sleep and dream.

▶ The two wrinkled hemispheres (halves) of the cerebrum, where thinking happens, are the largest brain parts.

The brain looks like a wrinkly lump of grey-pink jelly! On average, it weighs about 1.4 kilograms. It doesn't move, but its amazing nerve activity uses up one-fifth of all the energy needed by the body.

Cerebral hemisphere

Thalamus

Hippocampus

Cerebellum

Brain stem

▼ Different areas or centres of the brain's outer layer, the cerebral cortex, deal with messages from and to certain parts of the body.

Touch area

Movement area

Thought area

Vision area

Hearing area

Speech area

The main part of the brain is its bulging, wrinkled upper part, the cerebrum. Different areas of its surface (cerebral cortex) deal with nerve signals to and from different parts of the body. For example, messages from the eyes pass to the lower rear part of the cerebrum, called the visual centre. They are sorted here as the brain cells work out what the eyes are seeing. There are also areas for touch, hearing, taste and other body processes.

The cerebellum is the rounded, wrinkled part at the back of the brain. It processes messages from the motor centre, sorting and coordinating them in great detail, to send to the body's hundreds of muscles. This is how we learn skilled, precise movements such as writing, skateboarding or playing music (or all three), almost without thinking.

The brain stem is the lower part of the brain, where it joins the body's main nerve, the spinal cord. The brain stem controls basic processes vital for life, like breathing, heartbeat, digesting food and removing wastes.

▲ Our brains allow us to draw from memory, expressing emotions.

The brain really does have 'brain waves'. Every second it receives, sorts and sends millions of nerve signals. Special pads attached to the head can detect these tiny electrical pulses. They are shown on a screen or paper strip as wavy lines called an EEG, electro-encephalogram.

▼ The brain's 'waves' or EEG recordings change, depending on whether the person is alert and thinking hard, resting, falling asleep or deeply asleep.

I DON'T BELIEVE IT!

The brain never sleeps! EEG waves show that it is almost as busy at night as when we are awake. It still controls heartbeat, breathing and digestion. It also sifts through the day's events and stores memories.

INDEX

ACKNOWLEDGEMENTS

All artworks are from the Miles Kelly Artwork Bank

The publishers would like to thank the following sources for the use of their photographs:

t = top, b = bottom, c = centre, l = left, r = right, m = main, bg = background

Cover (front) 2012 American Honda Motor Co. Inc., (spine) courtesy of Apple (back) Silverstore/Dreamstime, Stephen Coburn/Fotolia, Andreas Meyer/Shutterstock (bg) ilolab/Shutterstock

Dreamstime 20 Silverstore; 21(bg) Adam1975; 23(t) Paha_l; 36(tr) Zoom-zoom; 89(b) Alangh; 90(b) Velkol; 105 Tobkatrina; 111 Kati1313; 123 Barsik

Fotolia 15(tl) Paul Heasman, (cr) Dariusz Kopestynski; 23(b) photlook; 36(third from tr); 50–51(tc) Alexey Khromushin; 56(b) Rafa Irusta; 63(b); 71(cr); 73(t); 74(cl); 79(br) scazza; 84(tl) U.P. images; 85(tr) Sharpshot; 99 chrisharvey; 101 Alexander Yakovlev; 119(r) Andres Rodriguez

Getty Images 39(b) Laguna Design

iStockphoto.com 18–19(bg) Kevin Smith; 58–59(bg) Sander Kamp; 65(br) Duncan Walker; 76(br) HultonArchive; 80(tl) hohos, 80(bl) James Steidl; 91(b) Rosemarie Gearhart

NASA 84(br) NASA Marshall Space Flight Center (NASA-MSFC); 85(bl) NASA Stennis Space Center, (br) NASA MSFC

Rex Features 75(c) Rex Features

Shutterstock 8–9 ssguy; 10–11 Sergey Lavrentev; 11(t) Ljupco Smokovski; 12(bg) Deymos, (tr) Vakhrushev Pavel, (b) Ivonne Wierink; 13(t) w shane dougherty; 14(tr) yuyangc; 16(m) yxm2008, (bl) ARENA Creative; 17(b) Tatiana Makotra; 22(bg) asharkyu, (cr) Eimantas Buzasl; 24–25(m) vadim kozlovsky; 26–27(bg) Gunnar Pippel; 26(b) Smileus; 27(c) Ray Hub; 28(c) Sebastian Crocker; 29(b) Hywit Dimyadi; 30–31(bg) archibald, (c) ifong; 31(tl) Viktor Gmyria; 32–33(bg) Redshinestudio; 33(all) Annette Shaff; 34 Jaggat; 35(c) michael rubin; 36(second from tr) Maksim Toome, (fourth from tr) Balazs Toth, CaptureLight, Jaochainoi; 43(t) wim claes, (b) indiangypsy; 44(m) beerkoff, (bl) Smit; 47(tr) Morgan Lane Photography, (b) ssuaphotos; 50–51(bg) Mark Carrel; 51(cr) Richard Peterson, (br) Fedorov Oleksiy; 52(tr) Marijus Auruskevicius; 53(tr) Maksym Gorpenyuk; 55(tl) Bernd Juergens, (br) Michael Stokes; 57(b) Orientaly; 59(c) Oleg - F, (r) Kjersti Joergensen; 61(br) Darren Baker; 62(l) Alex Staroseltsev; 65(bl) K. L. Kohn; 66(t) Awe Inspiring Images; 67(c) Galushko Sergey, (bc) Indigo Fish, (tr) Ispace; 68(bl) Geoffrey Kuchera; 69(t) Alexandru Chririac; 71(tl) marekuliasz, (bl) Lim Yong Hian; 72(tl) alexnika; 73(m) Caitlin Mirra; 74(violas) Milan Vasicek; (conductor) HitToon.com; 75(br) Stephen Meese; 76(l) EW CHEE GUAN, (cr) Barry Barnes, (b) Pakhnyushcha; 77(br) Galushko Sergey Alekseewisch; 78–79(m) Becky Stares; 79(tr) c.; 81(cl) Gordan, (bl) drfelice; 83(t) Maksym Bondarchuk, (bl) steamroller_blues, (br) Slaven; 84–85(bg) plavusa87; 86–87 jan kranendonk; 86(tl) fotoluminate, (tl) Jurgen Ziewe; 89(cl) Anneka; 91(t) Kozlovskaya Ksenia; 92 Lilya Espinosa; 93 Stanislav Fridkin; 94(blonde) Jeanne Hatch, (straight black) wong sze yuen, (curly black) Felix Mizioznikov; 95(l) Steven Chiang, (r) Carmen Steiner; 98 konmesa; 102–103 PiLart; 102 Taranova; 103 Jaren Jai Wicklund; 104 JonMilnes; 107 Lawrence Wee; 108–109 Elena Schweitzer; 108(bl) Yuri Arcurs; 111 Kati1313; 114–115(bg) Sebastian Kaulitzki; 117(tr) beerkoff; 119(l) Paul Matthew Photography; 121 Elena Elisseeva; 125 Sebastien Burel

All other photographs are from: digitalSTOCK, digitalvision, John Foxx, PhotoAlto, PhotoDisc, PhotoEssentials, PhotoPro, Stockbyte

Every effort has been made to acknowledge the source and copyright holder of each picture. Miles Kelly Publishing apologises for any unintentional errors or omissions.